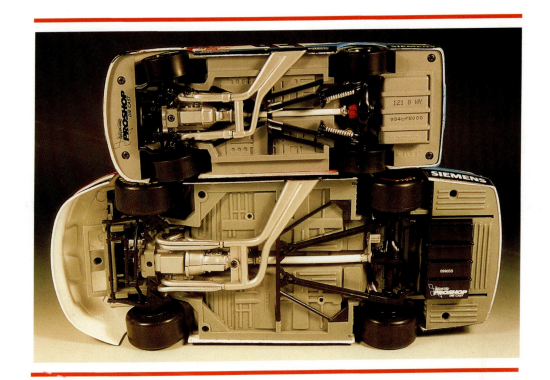

NASCAR
DIECAST AND MODEL CARS

BILL COULTER

MBI Publishing Company

First published in 2001 by MBI Publishing Company, Galtier Plaza, Suite 200, 380 Jackson Street, St. Paul, MN 55101-3885 USA

© Bill Coulter, 2001

All rights reserved. With the exception of quoting brief passages for the purposes of review, no part of this publication may be reproduced without prior written permission from the Publisher.

The information in this book is true and complete to the best of our knowledge. All recommendations are made without any guarantee on the part of the author or Publisher, who also disclaim any liability incurred in connection with the use of this data or specific details.

We recognize that some words, model names and designations, for example, mentioned herein are the property of the trademark holder. We use them for identification purposes only. This is not an official publication.

MBI Publishing Company books are also available at discounts in bulk quantity for industrial or sales-promotional use. For details write to Special Sales Manager at Motorbooks International Wholesalers & Distributors, Galtier Plaza, Suite 200, 380 Jackson Street, St. Paul, MN 55101-3885 USA.

About the Author
Bill Coulter has been a freelance writer since the 1970s and his articles have appeared in magazines such as *Scale Model Enthusiast*, *Circle Track*, *AutoWeek*, and *Model Cars*. Coulter currently owns and operates a consulting business that specializes in the design and development of sales and marketing materials. Coulter, and his wife, Gail, live in Xenia, Ohio. This is Coulter's seventh book.

Library of Congress Cataloging-in-Publication Data
Coulter, Bill.
    NASCAR diecast and model cars / Bill Coulter.
        p. cm. — (Nostalgic treasures)
    Includes index.
    ISBN 0-7603-0980-9 (pbk.: alk. paper)
    1. Automobiles, Racing—Models—Collectors and collecting. I. Title. II. Series.

TL2372.C68.2001
629.2218—dc21   2001030731

Edited by Amy Glaser
Designed by Ole VonOlson

Printed in Hong Kong

Contents

Acknowledgments		.6
Introduction:	...The Scope of NASCAR Collectibles	.7
Chapter 1	.....Building and Collecting Issues	.11
Chapter 2	.....Manufacturer Profiles	.19
Chapter 3	.....How Plastic Kits and Diecast Models Are Made	.29
Chapter 4	.....Petty Enterprises	.35
Chapter 5	.....Hendrick Motorsports	.43
Chapter 6	.....Richard Childress Racing/Dale Earnhardt, Inc.	.53
Chapter 7	.....Robert Yates Racing	.63
Chapter 8	.....Roush Racing	.75
Chapter 9	.....Penske Racing	.85
Chapter 10	.....Joe Gibbs Racing	.93
Chapter 11	.....Bill Davis Racing	.101
Chapter 12	.....Evernham Motorsport	.107
Chapter 13	.....Alan Kulwicki Racing	.113
Value Guide		.116
Index		.127

Acknowledgments

No project such as this can be undertaken without the unselfish cooperation of a variety of individuals. During the months I spent preparing this manuscript, a core group of dedicated collectors and builders gave me access to their collections of diecast, unbuilt kits, and highly prized, built stock car models. Without these cherished collectible items, the images in this book would have been minimal. Those people contributing to this effort include: Mike Petrose, John Barton, John Coulter, Leonard Carsner, Fred Bradley, Mike Madlinger, Andrew Madlinger, Wayne Doebling, Wayne Moyer, Daryl Huhtala, Tom Dill, Norman DeHaven, and Rob Shelton.

These fine folks provided unlimited access to their collections and shared their insights and advice on many occasions. Thanks to Drew Hierwarter and Garry McWhirter for their photo images of many of today's top stock car racing personalities. I would also like to thank the spokespersons for various manufacturers who took time to answer my questions and provided me with in-depth information about their products and company histories. Special thanks go to Tom Long for his photos of diecast manufacturing, and also to Bob Johnson for various plastic kit manufacturing photos.

Introduction: The Scope of NASCAR Collectibles

NASCAR-related, pre-assembled diecast replicas and plastic model kits are the hot ticket in motorsports collectibles today. Although the two product types have a lot in common, they have each come to this position by different routes. For diecast models, this is a relatively recent phenomenon dating back to the early 1990s. Plastic model kits of NASCAR stock cars went through a major rebirth in the early 1980s.

Today, NASCAR collectibles are sold at racetracks, online, by mail order, and at every type of retail outlet. Display advertisements for these products are found in just about every major publication, from *TV Guide* to *Motor Trend* magazine. Monthly price guide publications, including *Beckett Racing & Motorsports Marketplace*, *Racing Collector's Price Guide*, and *Die Cast Digest*, monitor the pulse of this burgeoning market. These magazines feature reports on new items and reviews of specific product lines, catalog each release, and state the value of virtually every product type by category and manufacturer. The book *Stock Car Model Kit Encyclopedia and Price Guide* highlights nearly 900 kits in a wide variety of scales and includes their values.

Many seasoned observers of this whole genre suggest that there are three distinct categories: souvenirs, memorabilia, and collectibles. These definitions clearly establish the hobby of collecting NASCAR diecast and plastic model kit products as a recent phenomenon.

A souvenir is defined as something that is a reminder of a place or event. These items would include things acquired during a vacation or while attending a special function. Generally, they are items of little to moderate cost. These are items generally not considered collectibles, but they represent special memories and therefore are too valuable to throw away. A race program, ticket stub, or a racing postcard would fall into this catagory.

The memorabilia category is considered by many to include accumulated items that were not originally thought to have great value. A race driver's gloves, part of a race car, a sponsor's product banner, or a postcard are all examples of such items. These are also items that never were manufactured for the express purpose of collecting.

The final category is collectibles. This group contains items manufactured for the sole purpose of being purchased as an addition to a collection of similar products. Today, this category includes an unending list of products that range in price from under $1 to well over $100. This group includes such diverse products as clothing, trading cards, commemorative plates, diecast and plastic model kits, stuffed toys, books, videotapes, and figurines, to name a few. Most of these items are made in quantities of tens of thousands.

The vast appeal of NASCAR racing, which has a following virtually around the world, helped create this gargantuan market for stock car–related products. In recent years statistics show nearly 10 million spectators attend major-league stock car races annually, while nearly 150 million households are tuned in to each live TV broadcast. Through the 1990s, NASCAR attendance increased nearly 70 percent and TV ratings for stock car events perennially rank right up there with all of the other professional sports. Most of the largest sporting events in the United States are NASCAR races. Seating at many of the nation's racetracks today exceeds 150,000.

Statistics prove there are no consumers today more loyal than NASCAR race fans. Whether it's household detergents, soft drinks, automotive finishes, home improvement centers, industrial equipment, or cheeseburgers, it is a proven fact that NASCAR fans spend money liberally, and they strongly

NASCAR DIECAST AND MODEL CARS

The Revell Collection created this pair of 1/18th-scale diecast replicas of Mark Martin's No. 6. The 1997 Valvoline T-Bird is on the left, and the 1997 Winn-Dixie BGN ride of Mark Martin is on the right.

favor companies with a serious involvement in the sport. This fact has not been lost on many multinational corporations bent on making a profit.

Plastic Model Kits

Since the early 1980s when plastic stock car model kits experienced a major rebirth, model kits have been a staple retail sales item and are available through many mail-order operations. For the stock car model kit builder, 1983 was a bellwether year. Monogram Models (known today as Revell-Monogram) was always known for high-quality products, but they had never released NASCAR kits. Monogram introduced four new 1/24th-scale Winston Cup stockers that became the foundation for the most successful plastic model kit series in the history of the NASCAR collectible model car hobby.

The first releases included two Fords and two Buicks: the Bill Elliott Melling and Dale Earnhardt Wrangler T-Birds, and Darrell Waltrip's Mountain Dew and Buddy Baker's Uno Regals. The Fords rode on an unbelievably accurate and detailed Banjo Matthews rear-steer chassis, while the Buicks featured a front-steer platform scaled down from a Mike Laughlin chassis. These four kits set off a virtual feeding frenzy for NASCAR model kits that has not subsided for nearly 20 years.

Over time, Revell-Monogram released dozens of kits in this series including many different Fords, Buicks, Oldsmobiles, Pontiacs, and Chevrolets. Nearly every driver has been represented in this series, including many Daytona 500 winners and NASCAR champions. As a direct result of Revell-Monogram's efforts, a new subculture sprang to life as enterprising aftermarket companies began producing thousands of building and detailing items for this series of plastic kits. This plethora included die-cut, photo-etched, cast-resin and white metal parts and pieces for bumper-to-bumper application. Many of these product lines continue to this day to be good sellers.

Tens of thousands of water-slide decals have been sold over the intervening years. Companies such as SLIXX, Fred Cady Design, Yesterdays, and Chimneyville continue to release an ever-increasing array of body graphics to allow modelers of all persuasions to build replicas of their favorite race cars. Of course, the availability of dozens of alternate decal sheets over the last 20 years has certainly fueled a steady debate over whether the kits sold the aftermarket parts or vice versa.

Today, interest in plastic scale-model stock car kits continues to be strong. With the introduction of new body styles and new manufacturers like Dodge into NASCAR racing, there is every reason to believe stock car model kit building and collecting will remain healthy for a long time. The stock car model kit juggernaut is a euphoric experience if model building is your thing. With the resurgence of stock car modeling, many people have rediscovered this time-honored hobby. Others discovered they possessed hidden talents and have developed consummate building skills. Countless other enthusiasts discovered they had neither the time nor talent to pursue building as a leisure-time activity. As an alternative, some just collected kits. For many others there was a rather large void eagerly waiting to be filled; that void was filled with diecast stock cars.

Diecast

At first, a few inexpensive diecast pieces began to appear in smaller scales (1/64th to 1/43rd) in the early 1980s. These items, originally aimed at kids, were very toy-like and were manufactured in fairly large quantities by Ertl, Matchbox, and Mattel. A few of these items are highly prized by today's collectors. Included in this category are product lines of small-scale slot cars such as the Tyco HO Hardees '85 Thunderbird.

NASCAR diecast in larger scales, especially 1/24th and 1/18th, began to appear on store shelves in the late 1980s from companies including Racing Champions and Ertl. In 1992, Revell introduced a moderately priced line of (primitive by today's standards) 1/24th-scale diecast models. Eventually this series, like those from Racing Champions, included all of the competing car makes and many of the notable drivers and teams.

It wasn't long before Action Performance, Matchbox, Racing Champions, and Georgia Marketing and Promotions (GMP) with their Peachstate brand, joined the market with a wider range of NASCAR-related products including race car transporters and other support vehicles.

Major players like Team Caliber, Action, Revell Collection (now part of Action), Mattel, Hasbro, Brookfield Collectors Guild (now part of Action), Racing Champions, Ertl/AMT (now part of Racing Champions), and GMP continue to compete for our attention today. Products are available in scales from 1/64th, 1/43rd, 1/32nd, 1/24th, and 1/18th. Prices range from under $1 to well over $100. Even the venerable Franklin Mint has joined the fray with an exclusive line of 1/24th-scale Richard Petty race car replicas.

This is a closer look at this whole "whirling dervish" called NASCAR diecast and model cars. Major manufacturers are profiled, and you'll also be more knowledgeable about where these products come from and how they are produced.

The best-of-the-best in NASCAR Winston Cup racing like the Hendrick, Roush, and Petty superteams will be examined. Personal profiles and career highlight information about your favorite drivers are provided to help you understand the current state of this market and how it affects how and what you collect and build. Tighten your belts and adjust your seat. This will be a fast ride and the traffic is heavy!

As you add to your collection, consider narrowing the focus. Start by picking a favorite driver, product sponsor, make of car, or common scale. Here are examples of Kenny Irwin's 1998 Havoline No. 28 displayed in four different scales.

1

Building and Collecting Issues

Getting Organized

Many stock car model collectors or builders had no particular objective in mind when they began buying the occasional stock car model kit or randomly picking up a diecast item here or there. Collections are started innocently enough with a few kits and a couple diecast race cars. Whether your purchases were on impulse or just plain "I like that one and I gotta have it," you probably find yourself surrounded with dozens of plastic kits and/or numerous diecast items, and you may begin to wonder how you got into this situation!

Collect What You Like

The first question to ask yourself is, "Am I collecting things I really like or do I believe that some day I'll be able to put my grandkids through college by selling this stuff?" Rule number one: buy things for your collection you really like! Don't be mislead into believing your unbuilt kit or diecast collection is somehow continually increasing in value like investing in annuities, stocks and bonds, or CDs. There is a major reason why the majority of the collectibles on the market for the last few years will not rapidly increase in value in the near future. It's very simple. Souvenirs and memorabilia items are valuable today primarily because they were never produced just to be collected. In years past, they were thrown away or lost, or children played with them and the items were damaged or broken. What resulted over time is that a few desirable items survived. Today, demand exceeds availability, and the value of these items continues to escalate.

In contrast, today's diecast models are made specifically to be collected. These items are made literally by the thousands in spite of the package labeling that may state "1 of 10,000." That package designation is accurate as far as it goes. In many cases, the item you paid handsomely for is in fact "1 of 10,000." It's true for this particular run of 10,000, but for some products, there will undoubtedly be many runs of 10,000 pieces before production finally ceases. In the future, how valuable can an item be when 750,000 were produced? Add to that the fact that virtually every one of them has been lovingly stored in its original box.

Special commemorative paint schemes have become the norm for the last few seasons. We've had special race car graphics promoting everything from the Olympics to movie premieres to a primary sponsor's ancillary product lines. In some ways it probably seems like a great idea. In other ways, it has resulted in many teams running four, six, or eight different paint schemes in a season. Some of these layouts have been readily identifiable, while others have resulted in a particular race car being virtually unrecognizable. Whatever the pros or cons, this approach has resulted in the sale of many additional plastic kits and diecast models.

Focus Your Collection

As you grow your collection, consider narrowing the focus. Start by picking a favorite driver, product sponsor, make of car, or scale.

I've been a longtime Richard Petty fan. I haven't collected everything that has had the number 43 on it, but I have managed to collect a wide range of miniature Petty stock cars over the last 30 years. I've worked hard to keep my collection tightly focused. I don't collect black and silver biplanes, flourescent red and blue Model T pickup trucks, or rainbow-colored HO electric train sets. I have become very particular about what I am willing to add to my collection. I refuse to collect any NASCAR diecast model not carrying the proper sponsor's product markings. I can't see the point in spending my money for a No. 2 "Rusty" (no Miller

NASCAR DIECAST AND MODEL CARS

You might consider collecting items that represent defunct or no longer existing race teams. I collect diecast and kits of the Bahari No. 30 Pennzoil Pontiac, driven by Michael Waltrip and Johnny Benson, in a variety of scales.

The No. 35 Tabasco-sponsored Pontiac didn't hang around long on the NASCAR WC circuit. There are many interesting, low-volume No. 35 diecast collectibles that are part of my collection, including these pieces by Revell Collection and Hot Wheels.

BUILDING AND COLLECTING ISSUES

identification)Taurus or a No. 8 "Dale Jr." (no Budweiser markings)\Monte Carlo.

Swapping and Trading

Once you've made the hard choices to "purify" your particular stock car model collection, consider the items that don't make the final cut as legitimate and valuable trading stock. By taking this step with your extra pieces, you will have opened up a whole new avenue. Swapping and trading with other collectors, whether one on one or via classifieds and mail order, can be enriching and worthwhile. You'll make some new collecting "buddies" and learn a bit more about what you're collecting and sharpen your perception of values and prices.

Theme Collections

An eye-catching and conversation-inspiring display can be created by selecting your favorite driver or corporate sponsor and assembling multiple scales of diecast models into a collection. If you add to this corresponding built and unbuilt plastic kits, it will make for a memorable exhibit.

In recent times I've been one who hasn't resisted taking my own advice. I have been concentrating on collecting No. 30 Pennzoil, John Deere, and Tabasco stock car models. Probably none of these items will ever reach the level of desirability of those for Jeff Gordon or Dale Earnhardt (Sr. and Jr.) diecast; however, at the same time, I have never paid a small fortune for any of these items. I have yet to seek out their current value in a price guide. That aspect has never been that important to me. I like the exclusivity of collecting things that are outside the mainstream. I have often found new pieces for these collections at discount prices, and I'll bet the total production for all these items combined was just naturally far lower than many other more popular subjects we could point to.

The Wise Collector

Another important issue is learning as much as you possibly can about the items you are collecting. The more you know, the less likely you are to waste your hard-earned money on overpriced and under-detailed merchandise. I'm often asked, what is the real difference between a $40 model and an $80 model? Details! You get the detail, fit, and finish you pay for.

One excellent way of obtaining that valuable knowledge is to pay close attention not so much to prices quoted in value guides, but to what kits and diecast are selling for through classified ads and at flea markets. Anyone can state a dollar figure in a price guide. The true value of any item is the amount of money someone will pay you for an item at the time of the final sale.

Protecting Your Collection

For whatever reason you collect NASCAR models, knowing the true value of your collection can be very important. What would you do if your collection was stolen or destroyed by fire or some other natural disaster? Once the value of your collection reaches a few hundred dollars, consult the person you buy your household insurance through. He or she may be able to attach a rider to your homeowner's or renter's policy that will cover the collection in the event of some misfortune. Your insurance provider may want you to compile a list of individual items with accurate dollar values. He or she also might ask for a few snapshots of your prized possessions.

Product Jargon

Every manufacturer of diecast collectibles has used a plethora of product category names. No two terms mean the same thing from one manufacturer's line to another's. A few companies use a degree of descriptive terminology in providing customers some idea of what it is they are considering purchasing, but for mass-market products, these terms are mostly used for sales and marketing purposes. Other manufacturers have used nearly two dozen product category titles that ultimately wind up being confusing. I asked seasoned diecast collector Mike Petrose what all of this jargon meant to him and what it should mean to you and me. According to Petrose, you shouldn't be ashamed to admit that you have no idea what many of these product names mean. In many cases, Petrose says, they are simply designed as a way of relabeling or repackaging products to reach as broad a market as possible. Petrose also points out that many of these mass-market diecast product categories don't exist today.

NASCAR DIECAST AND MODEL CARS

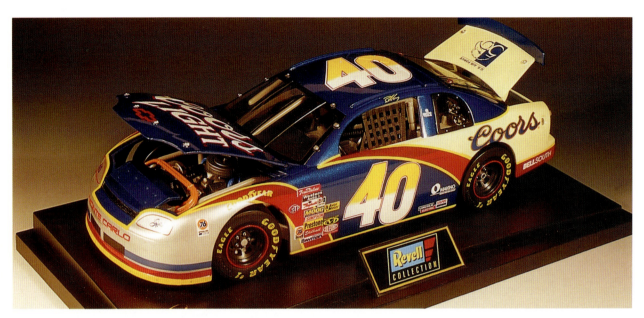

In the early 1980s, anybody could purchase a plastic kit of Bill Elliott's Coors-sponsored T-Bird. When Robby Gordon was signed to drive for Team Sabco in the mid-1990s, items such as this No. 40 Coors-sponsored Chevy (first release from Revell Collection) could only be sold as an "adult collectible."

Tobacco- and beer-sponsored diecast collectibles like this 1/18th-scale Revell Collection No. 33 Skoal Monte Carlo are firmly fastened to the display base by nonstandard hardware. Supposedly, this makes it even more of an "adult collectible," as reflected by the $100 price.

BUILDING AND COLLECTING ISSUES

"Action Performance has been good about maintaining consistent terminology for their product categories. Other manufacturers have very few categories, making it much easier to understand. For top-of-the-line products, there's Action Performance's Elite Series; Team Caliber has their Owner's Series; there are the Hot Wheels Crew's Choice and Ertl's Authentics as examples," Petrose said. In the case of Team Caliber, they've really kept it simple. The Owner's Series has all the bells and whistles such as a working suspension. Of course, the Preferred Series is less expensive and has fewer working parts. Like the old adage says, you get just what you pay for, and diecast collectibles are no different. These high-end products won't be found in mass-market retail stores like Wal-Mart, Kmart, and Toys "R" Us. The best a manufacturer has to offer can only be purchased from collectible and hobby shops or by mail order.

What Is RCCA?

The Racing Collectibles Club of America (RCCA) began in Georgia nearly 12 years ago. The club's first offerings were exclusive 1/64th-scale vintage stock cars. Action Performance purchased RCCA about 10 years ago. Today RCCA has over 150,000 members and offers exclusive items to their club members. "There was a separate Revell Collection Club prior to the Action Performance buyout. Their membership was absorbed into the RCCA. Revell Collection products included exclusive items for the 'club' membership and separate 'retail' pieces for sale to the general public. They were basically the same products, with the club piece having a sequential serial number," according to Petrose.

Politically Correct

Today, being politically correct (PC) is rampant even with NASCAR model kits and diecast collectibles. Alcohol- and tobacco-sponsored diecast items, branded as "Adult Collectibles," are usually at the high end of the price range ($50 to $100) and are usually sold by dealers and vendors at the track. Mass-market items in the $1 to $15 range don't make the cut most of the time, and are found at places like Wal-Mart and Toys "R" Us. The fear of alcohol- and beer-sponsored model kits and diecast falling into the hands of children, luring them into a life filled with alcohol and tobacco abuse, is highly suspect.

The rigid perception of today's societal movers and shakers is that ANY plastic model kit or inexpensive diecast is intended for children, even though hobby manufacturers' marketing research tells them the vast majority of collectors and builders today are adults. It's not that manufacturers wouldn't love to recapture the interest of today's kids, but so far it isn't happening. It also remains a fact that no statistical information exists in any way to link the building or collecting of scale-model stock cars sponsored by alcohol or tobacco products to the use of those products by children.

Oddly enough, there are no restrictions on children watching racing on TV or occupying pricey seats at stock car events underwritten by beer and tobacco companies. Children are also not restricted from wearing beer- or tobacco-related hats, T-shirts, and jackets. However, if children wish to build a scale model of the Skoal, Miller, Budweiser, or Coors race cars, they are out of luck. It will be interesting to see how many Mark Martin No. 6 Viagra-sponsored model kits and diecast cars are found in the nation's hobby shops and on Wal-Mart racks in 2001. Fortunately, in spite of this PC world of ours, manufacturers are currently producing plastic model kits and diecast replicas that are dead-on accurate.

Licensing

A major issue governing the stock car kit and diecast model business today is licensing fees. Licensing (the legal authorization to use the name or likeness of a driver, corporate sponsor, or make of automobile) allows manufacturers to legally produce specific racing-related products. A few years ago, all a manufacturer needed to do was contact a race team and request permission to produce a replica of one of their race cars. In exchange for a few cases of models, permission was generally granted. In those days a driver, corporate sponsor, or race team saw the benefits of using the packaged product as a promotional device and would quickly OK the deal.

Currently, plastic stock car kits can retail for as much as $25 each. Some high-end diecast models already top the $100 mark, and expect that price to continue to rise over time. If you ask why the price is so high, add royalties of 10 to 20 percent of the retail price, or more, to the development

NASCAR DIECAST AND MODEL CARS

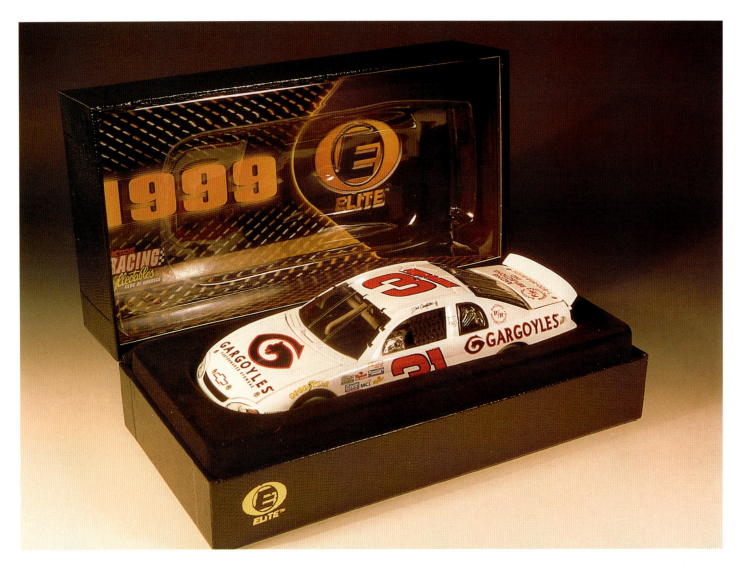

This 1/24th-scale No. 31 Gargoyles Chevy diecast model is typical of the Action Performance Elite series and is an exclusive item for RCCA club members.

BUILDING AND COLLECTING ISSUES

and production costs of $100,000 to $150,000, and you can see why new products are increasingly expensive.

I'd like to leave some final reminders about collecting NASCAR diecast and model cars: build and collect NASCAR models you really like; focus on a theme for your collection; learn all you can about what you're buying so you don't get snookered; insure your valuable NASCAR plastic kit and diecast collection; and above all, take pride in a very worthwhile hobby!

What Is Scale?

Nearly every diecast and plastic model kit found in this book falls into one of a number of precise scales. The following chart clearly shows the relationship between the dimensions of the full-size race car and its miniature counterpart. The scale fraction is followed by the comparison of what 1 inch on the model represents on the full-size race car.

Scale Breakdown

Scale	On model	Full size
1/144th	is 1 inch	= 144 inches
1/87th	is 1 inch	= 87 inches
1/64th	is 1 inch	= 64 inches
1/43rd	is 1 inch	= 43 inches
1/32nd	is 1 inch	= 32 inches
1/25th	is 1 inch	= 25 inches
1/24th	is 1 inch	= 24 inches
1/16th	is 1 inch	= 16 inches
1/12th	is 1 inch	= 12 inches
1/8th	is 1 inch	= 8 inches

Team Caliber is a relatively new company, but it has already established itself as a source of high-quality diecast collectibles. This 1/24th-scale 1999 STP/Petty Pontiac is a prime example of Team Caliber's quality craftsmanship.

2

Manufacturer Profiles

There are currently dozens of companies busily engaged in developing, marketing, and manufacturing NASCAR collectibles of virtually every description. Among these is a small cadre of suppliers of quality NASCAR diecast and plastic model kits. That number in some cases has decreased with the phenomenal expansion of the collectibles market, mostly due to mergers and acquisitions. This consolidation has had the effect, however, of enhancing the product development, engineering, and production side of the business.

Here is a closer look at a few of the time-tested players in this fascinating business of providing us with NASCAR diecast and plastic model kits.

Action Performance

Ohio native Fred Wagenhals started the Action Performance company in 1992. In the early 1990s, Wagenhals foresaw the huge business potential in the growing demand for NASCAR and other motorsports collectibles. Shortly thereafter, he launched this new enterprise as a dedicated diecast collectibles operation to specifically provide the race fan/customer with quality licensed merchandise.

Quickly, Action Performance (AP) became a major player in this rapidly expanding market. In the ensuing years, AP was able to expand its distribution networks to supply racing-related merchandise to a broader marketplace. By 1995, AP was firmly established as one of the leading sources for the most popular diecast products due to their aggressive pursuit of the leading personalities in NASCAR. AP continues to enjoy solid customer loyalty by maintaining price stability for its core products with complete lines ranging from $10 for their 1/64th-scale cars to $85 for their high-end collectible 1/24th-scale items.

One way that AP has continued to grow is through timely acquisitions. The first of these was Racing Collectibles, Inc., a nationwide wholesale diecast marketing firm. Next came Racing Collectibles Club of America (RCCA), a mail-order collector's merchandise club with a membership of 15,000 in 1993. Currently, RCCA has grown to over 165,000 satisfied collectors.

In 1996, AP purchased Sport Image, Inc., a leading motorsports merchandising firm from Dale Earnhardt, owner of the firm. As part of this transaction, AP signed Earnhardt to a 15-year licensing agreement. Included in the Sports Image deal was a small fleet of four semi-trucks and their 40-foot merchandise trailer, used for trackside retail sales. Today, the truck fleet includes over 20 rigs, a virtual franchise of rolling retail stores.

In 1997, AP acquired Charlotte-based Motorsports Traditions. With this transaction AP acquired exclusive rights to collectible products bearing the name, likeness, and signature of Jeff Gordon. Since then AP has acquired many other foreign and domestic companies including Brookfield Collectors Guild, Inc., a Wisconsin-based company that produces motorsports collectibles. In Europe, AP purchased Minichamps, who are best known for their quality sports racing and Formula 1 diecast products. After maintaining its headquarters in Phoenix, Arizona, for many years, AP recently relocated their operation to Charlotte, North Carolina—the acknowledged center of the stock car racing world. The AP website, goracing.com, receives 60 million hits per month.

Ertl/AMT

The name AMT came from the original company name Aluminum Model Toy. The new company began producing

NASCAR DIECAST AND MODEL CARS

In the late 1980s and early 1990s, Ertl was one of the first manufacturers to offer 1/18th-scale diecast stock cars as part of their American Muscle series. Shown here is the Mark Martin No. 6 T-Bird.

For a short period during the early 1990s, Ertl/AMT attempted to compete with Revell-Monogram with a series of 1/25th-scale plastic glue kits, including this pair of STP/Petty items.

metal promotional models in 1947, but switched over to injection molded plastic. AMT is credited with establishing the widely accepted 1/25th scale in the United States when their first 3-in-1 annual kit was introduced in 1958. The unusual scale came to be when 1/10th-scale auto factory–supplied blueprints were reduced 2.5 times to produce a model that would fit into a standard size promo box. AMT was always known for its extensive line of injection-molded plastic car kits which permitted early stock car model builders to replicate miniature versions of the race cars that were competing on the nation's racetracks.

AMT remained a worldwide leader and a major influence in automotive model kits until Matchbox/Lesney of Great Britain purchased the company in 1978. From that point on, the kit box logo reflected the new acquisition with the use of the AMT/Matchbox icon. When Lesney went

MANUFACTURER PROFILES

bankrupt in early 1982, the Ertl company of Iowa came to the rescue and acquired all the steel tools, injection molding machines, and rights to the high-visibility product line name.

In the early 1990s, Ertl/AMT was one of the first companies to produce large-scale diecast stock cars as part of their very successful American Muscle line. Ertl had concentrated on 1/18th scale until their acquisition by Racing Champions, Inc. In 1999, the Ertl/AMT diecast line expanded to include 1/64th- and 1/24th-scale stock cars under their Pro Shop brand name. In 1999, Racing Champions acquired the assets of Ertl/AMT in Dyersville, Iowa. Racing Champions Ertl continues to produce injection-molded plastic kits and NASCAR diecast stock car models from their Iowa facilities.

Georgia Marketing and Promotions

In 1992 what we now call "NASCAR diecast collectibles" were in their infancy. Tom Long, founder and president of GMP/Peachstate, quickly noted that items for the Busch Grand National (BGN) series teams and drivers were virtually nonexistent. Long drew up some contracts and headed for Charlotte, North Carolina, with plans to fill that void. Long signed up a number of BGN teams and drivers with agreements to replicate their transporters.

Next, Long approached the Ertl company hoping to enlist them as the manufacturer for GMP/Peachstate. Just when Long was ready to proceed, Ertl backed out, citing a conflict with another customer. It appeared that Long had a handful of contracts but no manufacturing capability.

By chance, Long met Stan Gill at a very crowded collectibles show in Daytona Beach, Florida. Long learned that Gill had just started a new company, Racing Collectibles, Inc. Gill had a new 1/64th-scale diecast mold for NASCAR transporters ready for production. Gill and Long joined forces, and GMP/Peachstate was in business!

When RCI was sold and became Action Performance, GMP/Peachstate decided to develop their own unique tooling. One of their first products was the Jeff Gordon/Baby Ruth BGN transporter. GMP/Peachstate has continued to expand this type of NASCAR-related collectibles line. Many of their earlier products have increased greatly in the secondary market. With a target production figure of between 2,500 and 3,500 pieces for each new product, it's no wonder that since its introduction virtually every item in the GMP/Peachstate line has been immediately gobbled up by an appreciative circle of customers.

Hasbro Winner's Circle

In 1923, brothers Henry and Helal Hassenfeld founded Hasbro, Inc., as a family-owned and -operated company to make pencil boxes and school supplies. In 75 years, the company has grown from a staff of just eight family members working in a small shop in Providence, Rhode Island, to a children's and family leisure-time entertainment company with over 10,000 employees around the world.

Hasbro is best known for innovative products for the American toy marketplace including Mr. Potato Head, which was introduced in the late 1940s, and G.I. Joe, which was released in 1964. In the 1980s it introduced such toy staples as Transformers and My Little Pony. By the mid-1980s Hasbro expanded by purchasing the assets of a number of smaller companies such as the Knickerbocker Toy Company, the Milton Bradley Company, and Ideal Games and Child Guidance products acquired from CBS.

Hasbro continued their expansion into the 1990s, particularly into several international markets which would eventually account for nearly 40 percent of the company's revenue. The year 1991 brought further expansion and acquisitions for Hasbro. The purchase of the Tonka Corporation brought Kenner Products and Parker Brothers divisions into the corporate fold. Now Hasbro was the parent company for such classic brands as Tonka Trucks, Monopoly, Nerf, Easy Bake, Clue, and Play-Doh products. By the late 1990s, Hasbro acquired other properties and companies, and developed a reputation as a leader in hand-held electronic and CD-ROM–based games through their new Hasbro Interactive division.

The Hasbro Winner's Circle NASCAR series is the best-selling brand of stock car–related scale vehicles, and reportedly holds a 52-percent market share in that category. The Winner's Circle brand was first introduced in 1997 and included products in 1/64th, 1/43rd, and 1/24th scales. Through a licensing partnership with Action Performance Co., Inc., Hasbro currently has agreements with many of the sport's premier drivers.

NASCAR DIECAST AND MODEL CARS

Hasbro's Winner's Circle brand was first introduced in 1997 and included products in 1/64th, 1/43rd, and 1/24th scales. Through a licensing partnership with Action Performance Co., Inc., Hasbro currently has agreements with many of the sport's premier drivers.

Nearly 20 years ago, Ertl offered this four-car set of 1981 NASCAR Buick Regals in 1/64th scale. Although these vehicles were mainly marketed to kids, the items quickly caught the eye of adult collectors.

MANUFACTURER PROFILES

Mattel/Hot Wheels

Mattel began business in 1945 as a small manufacturer of dollhouse furniture. From its humble beginnings, Mattel has grown to become a major global leader in manufacturing toys, dolls, and games, most notably Barbie dolls, Hot Wheels diecast cars, and Fisher-Price toys and games. Mattel currently employs over 26,000 people in 22 countries around the globe. Their customers come from all age groups in more than 65 countries.

Mattel introduced their Hot Wheels diecast car in 1968. Since then, the company has produced over two billion miniature cars, which greatly exceeds even the combined output of Detroit's Big Three. Mattel's initial involvement in NASCAR Winston Cup (WC) racing started in 1997 when they became the primary sponsor of the No. 44 Hot Wheels Pontiac driven by Kyle Petty. The company concentrated on mass-market product lines in 1/64th scale. The initial release comprised over 20 of the series' top drivers and cars. These deluxe models were targeted directly toward the adult collector and featured metal chassis and bodies with two-piece wheels and tire sets. Similar items utilizing less expensive materials were targeted toward children for use with their Hot Wheels tracks.

In 1998, Mattel expanded their NASCAR lines to include 1/43rd- and 1/24th-scale models, 1/64th-scale transporters, and the Pit Crew and War Wagon series which combine a car with team-specific accessories. Since 1999, Mattel has continued to build on their extensive line of stock car–related products. These include hobby shop–quality replicas with increased detail like their Select, NASCAR Rocks, and Crew's Choice series. In 2000, the Radical Rides and Treasure Hunt series were released.

Monogram Models, Inc.

Monogram Models, Inc. (MMI) was the brainchild of Bob Reder and Jack Besser in late 1945 near Chicago, Illinois. The partners began manufacturing balsa wood kits of World War II warships. After manufacturing wooden kits for a while, the company quickly switched to injection-molded plastic by the early 1950s. In 1954, Monogram introduced their first all-plastic model car kit, No. P-1, the Midget Racer. It wasn't long before the demand for similar kits led Reder and Besser to the decision to produce nothing but injection-molded plastic model kits.

The whole plastic hobby kit business virtually exploded at this point, and Monogram was riding the crest of the wave. What followed was a veritable history of contemporary American civilization as reflected in the automotive kit subject material. Monogram has always been noted for its high quality and diverse product mix. Today a company spokesperson is quick to confess that model car subjects now account for over 60 percent of their business.

In 1968 Monogram was purchased by Mattel, Inc., the world's largest toy manufacturer. At first, Mattel took control of all product development, marketing, and sales for the Monogram plastic kit line. Some observers believe that the parent company tried to turn Monogram Models into a toy company. When this new approach didn't work and sales began to decline sharply, Mattel (in 1972) returned product development, marketing, and sales back to the Monogram staff.

The entire domestic hobby business suffered a "shake-up" when hand-held and parlor electronic games were introduced. Of course, U.S. economic conditions were also in a mild recession. Mattel was experiencing cash-flow problems because their type of hand-held, battery-operated video games were not selling. For Monogram, funding for new tooling was drastically cut, forcing them to concentrate on revising and converting older tooling into new products.

Economic conditions began improving in 1983. Bob Johnson, Monogram's risk-taking product manager, proposed the development of a totally new line of NASCAR-style stock car model kits. The first four releases in the series included two Ford Thunderbirds and two Buick Regals. Johnson, who has since left Monogram to start his own hobby kit company, says, "those four releases put Monogram on the map as a serious manufacturer of stock car model kits for all time." Since their introduction in 1983, dozens of different superspeedway race cars have been produced including Fords, Chevrolets, Buicks, Oldsmobiles, and Pontiacs. "You're probably looking today at a model kit series that has produced more than 3 to 4 million pieces," adds Johnson with a smile. Reliable sources confirm that the stock car line has become a mainstay to Monogram's bottom line each year since its introduction.

NASCAR DIECAST AND MODEL CARS

Mattel's Hot Wheels brand had its first involvement with NASCAR in 1997 when Hot Wheels agreed to sponsor Kyle Petty's No. 44 Pontiac. Although Hot Wheels makes diecast stock cars in a variety of scales, these small subjects remain very popular with collectors, including these four Petty family sets.

In 1984, Tom Gannon (former MMI president) and a group of investors successfully purchased Monogram from Mattel. The company continued to grow and expand its product line, and by mid-1986, Odyssey Partners (an investment group) purchased Monogram. Shortly after that acquisition, Odyssey also acquired the assets of Revell, Inc., which surveys had shown was still the most recognized name in the hobby business. In 1995, Revell-Monogram, Inc., was purchased by Binney & Smith, owners of Hallmark greeting cards and Crayola crayons. R-M is comfortably positioned the leisure-time consumer products division with these other highly visible product groups.

Racing Champions Ertl

In 1989, Bob Dods, Boyd Meyer, and Peter Chung coordinated their collective experience as toy manufacturer sales representatives, combined that with the rapid growth and popularity of NASCAR, and launched a new company, Racing Champions. The new company's initial products consisted of a line of toy-like stock car diecast models. Over the intervening years, Racing Champions focused on expanding and diversifying their product lines while continuing to develop affordable automotive and racing collectibles.

In June 1998, Racing Champions acquired Wheels Sports Group, which included the leading brand of NASCAR trading cards, Press Pass, and Wheels. This merger broadened the scope of Racing Champions' NASCAR collectibles and expanded the distribution channels for their unique line of stock car diecast replicas.

In 1999, Racing Champions acquired the assets of Ertl/AMT in Dyersville, Iowa. One of the oldest and most respected names in collectibles, Ertl was founded in 1945 by Fred Ertl Sr. For many years Ertl was known as a leader in manufacturing agricultural diecast and plastic commercial transportation model kits. Ertl acquired all the steel tools, injection-molding machines, and rights to the high-visibility product line name when AMT's British parent company, Lesney Products (Matchbox), went bankrupt in early 1982.

MANUFACTURER PROFILES

Today, the Ertl division of Racing Champions Ertl is a market leader in both agricultural and custom imprint diecast collectibles. The new company, Racing Champions Ertl, continues to produce AMT injection-molded plastic kits and NASCAR diecast stock car models with offices in Glen Ellyn, Illinois; Dyersville, Iowa; Charlotte, North Carolina; and Hong Kong, China.

Beginning in the early 1990s, Ertl/AMT was one of the first companies to produce large-scale diecast stock cars as part of their very successful American Muscle line. Ertl had concentrated on 1/18th scale until their acquisition by Racing Champions, Inc. In 1999, the Ertl/AMT diecast line was expanded to include 1/64th- and 1/24th-scale stock cars under their Pro Shop brand name. Racing Champions Ertl currently has permanent product displays in more than 20,000 retail locations, including mass merchant retailers such as Wal-Mart, Kmart, Target, and Toys "R" Us, in addition to regional and specialty retailers and hobby stores nationwide.

NASCAR diecast replicas remain one of the cornerstones of Racing Champions Ertl under both the Racing Champions and the Ertl American Muscle brand names. Today, the company offers stock car models in three scales with a suggested price range between $2 and $60.

Revell, Inc.

Lew Glaser started Revell in California just before World War II. Eventually Revell would become the largest manufacturer of plastic kits in the world. The Revell logo proved, over the years, to be the most recognizable in the hobby business. Revell's first all-plastic model car kit was a 1/16th-scale 1910 Maxwell, released in 1951.

Revell remained a wholly American-owned company until 1979 when French toy producer Compagnie Generale Du Jouet acquired the company assets. In 1986, Odyssey Partners, owners of Monogram Models, Inc., bought the Revell company. All physical assets were phased out in Venice, California, and moved to Des Plaines, Illinois, a short distance from the Monogram facilities in nearby Morton Grove.

There were no stock car model kits produced under the Revell brand name until the Monogram acquisition. The 1/25th-scale American Speed Association (ASA) stock car kit

The brand names Monogram, Revell-Monogram, and Revell have graced product packaging, as seen with this No. 97 John Deere Pontiac. Whatever brand name is used, it's still an excellent line of 1/24th-scale plastic glue kits from the Morton Grove, Illinois, manufacturer.

series was Revell's first and only venture into the oval track racer hobby market until the company retired the Monogram brand name. This was the result of a corporate edict at the time that said competing product lines, Monogram and Revell, could not offer the same type of model kits. Currently, the Revell brand name has become the dominant one for this company's combined product line and remains a part of the Hallmark division of Binney & Smith.

Revell Collection

What eventually became Revell Collection started out as a small company, SMSC. In the early 1990s, this new company joined with Stan and Andy Gill, who founded Racing Collectibles Club of America (RCCA), to produce racing collectibles that could be sold at the race track. SMSC functioned as an agent for RCCA, which employed Deles International (noted diecast manufacturer) in Hong Kong, China. SMSC's Dick and Jan Nelson were the primary per-

NASCAR DIECAST AND MODEL CARS

Shown here are two 1/24th-scale Action Performance diecast models of cars driven by the Sr. and Jr. Earnhardts in a NASCAR nonpoints race at Twin Ring Motegi, Japan, in 1998.

sonnel in this small company. Together they conducted research and development to eventually perfect a computerized method for transferring the technical artwork to Deles.

By the mid-1990s, Action Performance purchased RCCA, citing an urgent need for experienced manufacturing capabilities. This relationship lasted only a few months and SMSC returned to doing premium diecast programs for major clients on its own. By 1996, Dick Nelson sought to align his company, SMSC, with a major hobby manufacturer as a self-preservation move. Companies, including Mattel, were approached. Georgia Marketing and Promotions' Tom Long hooked Nelson up with Carl Pickard from Revell. Shortly thereafter, Revell bought the assets of SMSC, which was renamed Revell Collection.

With a business plan and a small staff, the new entity opened an office in Charlotte, North Carolina. Included among the RC players were Dick Nelson, president; Bob Johnson, designer; Suzi Lewis, product distribution; and Ed Eidam, general manager.

The Revell Collection line quickly became the fastest growing division of the company. Revell Collection received corporate parent Binney & Smith's President's Award in their second year of operation. In just two years the Revell Collection accounted for over $20 million in sales. In 1998, the assets of Revell Collection were acquired by Action Performance. One year later, many of the same people banded together to start Team Caliber.

MANUFACTURER PROFILES

Team Caliber

Team Caliber, located in Charlotte, North Carolina, is a small company that started business just over three years ago. It's a group of knowledgeable people led by general manager Randy Duncan, who literally hit the "track" in high gear. Many of TC's personnel can trace their roots in the diecast business back to Revell Collection and other collectibles operations. This new company quickly set extremely high product standards in the NASCAR diecast marketplace. The group of core talent at Team Caliber is made up of people who already knew how to get the job done right.

IRT Design in Charlotte, North Carolina, is the primary product development source for Team Caliber. This is the same organization responsible for developing the Revell Collection product line. IRT gathers the research information, generates the design work, and interprets that information to successfully coordinate efforts with the best diecast manufacturing facilities, which are located in the Far East.

Team Caliber concentrates on the high-dollar, high-quality, high-end segment of the market. They have two 1/64th-scale product lines as well. Limited production figures for 1/24th-scale replicas range from 3,120 to 5,004 pieces. For the 1/64th-scale cars, edition production runs from 7,000 to 10,080. Team Caliber's piggy banks are subject to even stricter production limits of no more than 1,008.

Roush Racing acquired Team Caliber in 2000. Team Caliber is currently an independent subsidiary of Roush Corporation, an automotive research and development giant. The Team Caliber, LLC web site address is www.teamcaliber.com.

Racing Champions began manufacturing diecast models in 1989. Some of their more notable products include these Petty items that were created in 1999 to commemorate the family operation's 50 years in racing.

A craftsman is making parts out of wood for a 1/10th-scale model kit master pattern

3
How Plastic Kits and Diecast Models Are Made

Since the late 1940s, scale-model kit manufacturers have used polystyrene plastic and injection molding technology to manufacture kits. This material and manufacturing process is responsible for literally millions of hobby kits produced since. In the late 1980s and into the early 1990s, diecast manufacturers employed a similar molding process which substitutes Zamak (a zinc and aluminum compound available in nuggets or ingots) for styrene plastic to produce rugged and durable products for an ever-expanding collectibles market. This process remains a time-consuming and expensive procedure, but currently there are no ready substitutes for this time-tested technology.

Concept and Design

Whether it's a plastic kit or a diecast product, it starts as a concept or idea, conceived by a group or an individual, that seems likely to be a good seller. Such things are never pursued on a notion or a whim. With tooling costs ranging from $100,000 to $200,000, the financial risks are very high. Only after weighing the risks against the possibility of great success does the manufacturer move forward in the process.

Next, a full-size race car is thoroughly measured and photographed from every possible angle. Engineers and designers then create a set of working drawings. Today, manufacturers capture this data in electronic files, which allows the tooling to be created by computer-driven (CNC) machine tool and die equipment. Also, a complete series of drawings are developed for even the smallest parts. This mound of technical data is then transferred to a team of skilled craftspeople who generate a series of three-dimensional mockups in wood and resin at 1/10th scale to create what is commonly called a "master." Each of these individual pieces faithfully represents every part of the full-size subject and will be used as a guide to engrave steel diework for each part on the finished scale model.

At this point, each part of the master or pattern piece goes to craftspeople responsible for cutting the final shapes into steel tooling. A pantograph machine is employed to mathematically reduce the size of each part from the 1/10th-scale master down to 1/18th, 1/24th, 1/32nd, 1/43rd, 1/64th, or whatever scale is desired for the final product. Convex and concave shapes are carefully cut into case-hardened steel blocks to form two-piece molds. There compose the final pieces from which the plastic kit or diecast model will be injection-molded.

Tooling

The finished dies are inserted into an injection-molding machine that is capable of forcing either liquid polystyrene or molten liquid Zamak into the molds under extremely high temperature and pressure. The initial runs of pieces are referred to as "test shots." These test shots are reviewed and checked repeatedly against the original data. Every effort is made to refine the final diework for accuracy, finish, alignment, and fit. An engraver cleans up the mold surfaces and polishes everything to a mirrorlike sheen to prepare for the production run. For plastic model kits, test shots are thoroughly reviewed by company engineers and designers, and often by the automotive manufacturer who licenses this type product to ensure that top quality is maintained. In the case of diecast models, as part of the final review prior to actual production, finished parts are assembled and presented to the race car driver, team, sponsor representatives, or automotive manufacturer for the final OK. Once everyone gives their approval, production begins.

NASCAR DIECAST AND MODEL CARS

Pictured here (clockwise) are a plaster mold made from the wood master, an assembly of inserts in a mold base, and a finished mold.

This injection-molding machine is really a 100-ton press. Shown in the foreground are parts that were just removed from the machine. From this angle we can see the two halves of the steel tooling along with the cooling tubes carrying glycanol (automotive antifreeze), which is used to quickly cool the mold to help ease the removal of each set of parts.

HOW PLASTIC KITS AND DIECAST MODELS ARE MADE

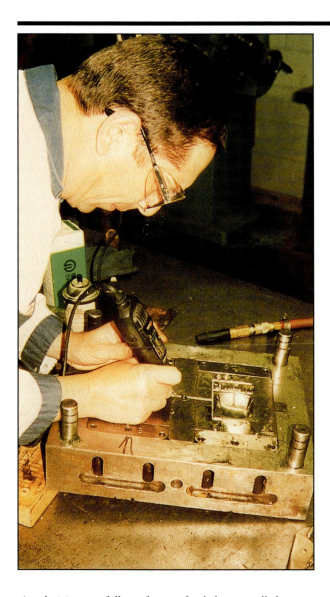

A technician carefully performs a final cleanup called "maintenancing" to a section of steel tooling before it heads for the injection-molding machine. He uses a high-speed grinding tool to remove excess materials, sharpen edges, or reform critical surfaces.

Manufacturing

Each plastic model kit begins as a drum of tiny granules. Various colors are blended together and heated to a fluid state in preparation for injection into the molds under extreme pressure. After the pieces are removed from the molding machine, all parts are inspected, cleaned, and prepared for painting, finishing, and final assembly. Each piece of Zamak is tumbled in finishing pellets and a slurry mixture to remove rough edges, and mold seams and parting lines. A liquid enamel paint is then applied to the electrically charged parts in a heated environment using the Randsburg electrostatic painting system. This is the same process used in the auto industry to apply paint to new cars.

Tampo or pad printing is used to apply all the scripts, badging, body graphics, numerals, and sponsors' decals onto the diecast model car body shell. Pad printing is an offset-style application process that allows for the imprinting of various multicolored images onto flat or compound surfaces.

The final manufacturing step is to bring all the contents of each kit together along an assembly line where the instruction sheet, decals, tires, and chrome and plastic parts join the remainder of the kit's plastic parts. The loaded kit box is shrink-wrapped and sent to the warehouse. From there, cases of kits are sent to distributors, wholesalers, and ultimately to resellers for sale to the public.

The parts of the kit that need to be plated are separated from the rest. The bright chromelike finish for these parts is achieved by using a process called "vacuum plating." First, the parts are attached to a cylindrical-style rack, sprayed with a clear lacquer, and inserted into a vacuum chamber. Here, all of the air is pumped out of the chamber and an electrical current is passed through pieces of aluminum that evaporate, literally exploding in all directions and coating the surface of everything inside the chamber.

Final assembly brings all of the finished parts and pieces together in one place. Human hands, working together along a rudimentary assembly line, carefully assemble all of the individual parts to produce finished diecast models. Assembled models are individually boxed, packed in crates, and shipped out. From here the product is channeled into the manufacturer's mail-order system or sent out to distributors, wholesalers, and resellers for sale to the general public.

NASCAR DIECAST AND MODEL CARS

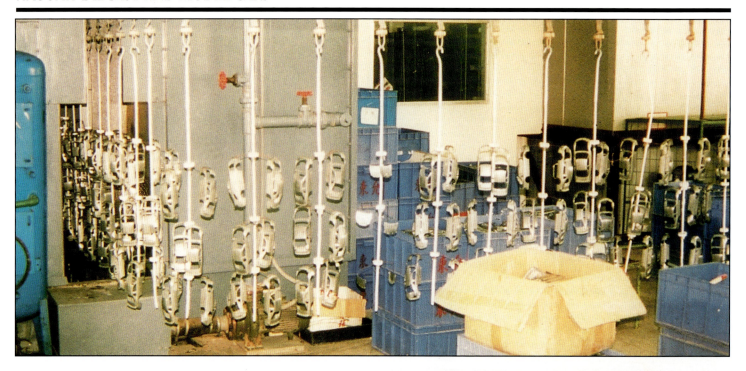

Diecast model car bodies have been mounted on a conveyor in preparation for the electrostatic painting process.

Here a worker is drilling a tap hole by hand in preparation for mounting an accessory to this transporter trailer.

HOW PLASTIC KITS AND DIECAST MODELS ARE MADE

The Investment

Producing a diecast scale model remains a costly and time-consuming process. Mistakes and delays can cripple a company's ability to stay in business for very long. Currently, steel-tooling diework to produce a scale diecast model costs from $150,000 to $250,000. The time from concept to finished product can be six to nine months. The requisite steel tooling is created in Canada and China. Most plastic kit production today takes place in North America. By contrast, most of the best diecast production facilities are offshore in locations such as Malaysia, Hong Kong, or mainland China.

These two workers are operating a styrene plastic injection-molding machine and are producing test shots of a new product.

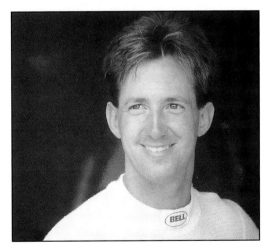

The late Adam Petty, the first fourth-generation athlete in the professional sports field.

John Andretti has driven just about everything with wheels. He seems firmly entrenched driving the No. 43 Cheerios Dodge in 2001.

Richard and Linda Petty in victory lane at Michigan International Speedway in September 1979.

4

Petty Enterprises

Arguably the most famous and respected family in motorsports celebrated their golden anniversary in racing in 1999. Little did the family patriarch, Lee Petty, realize 50 years ago when he began racing what an unbelievable chain of events were being set into motion. Any discussion of NASCAR racing logically begins with the Petty family.

Since entering NASCAR racing in 1949, the Petty Enterprises facilities in Level Cross, North Carolina, have grown from a single converted reaper shed with a dirt floor to an expansive state-of-the-art racing operation covering thousands of square feet. From a one-car operation with only family and friends as crew members, Petty Enterprises' Level Cross operation now has dozens of employees. Today, this facility is home to two Pontiac Winston Cup (WC) teams for John Andretti and Kyle Petty, a Chevrolet Busch Grand National (BGN) team, and a single Dodge pickup team that competes full-time in the Craftsman Truck Series (CTS). The Petty Museum on the grounds of the Petty Enterprises compound also is host to thousands of visitors each year, and offers many examples of the famous Petty race cars. The Petty Driving Experience is a fixture at such hallowed facilities as Charlotte, Daytona, and Las Vegas speedways. You have the option of taking a three-lap ride at speed in the passenger seat or signing on for a full course that includes classroom instruction and solo driving stints.

Lee Petty

Lee Petty didn't start racing full-time until he was 35 years old. Most of today's successful drivers aren't even 30 years old yet. Lee's career was a glorious one, although it was much too brief. It is amazing that during this period (1949–1964), the senior Petty won 54 races and was series champion in 1954, 1958, and 1959. Like so many early pioneers of the sport of stock car racing, Lee Petty is responsible for building the solid foundation that, along with legendary NASCAR founder Bill France Sr.'s efforts, set the stage for public acceptance and phenomenal growth. Lee retired from driving to manage the family operation full-time in 1964. Eventually Lee Petty retired from the family business in the mid-1980s to play golf on a daily basis. He died at the age of 86 on April 5, 2000, from a stomach aneurysm.

Richard Petty

Lee refused to allow his eldest son Richard to consider a driving career until he was 21. When Richard was 18, he asked his father if he could race and received an emphatic "no" as his answer about continuing the family legacy. As Richard continued to serve as his father's chief mechanic, his desire to drive competitively never subsided. When Richard turned 21, he asked his father about driving once more. Lee never stopped what he was doing and simply motioned toward a well-worn 1957 Oldsmobile sitting in the corner of the shop. Richard fixed up that Oldsmobile and entered in his first race in 1958. One of the greatest careers in racing was launched from these very humble beginnings. From his first race in Ontario, Canada, to his first of 200 career victories at the now defunct Charlotte, North Carolina, dirt track, Richard Petty has become a living legend with a legion of fans in virtually every country around the globe.

Kyle Petty

Richard and Linda Petty's only son, Kyle, started his racing career with a bang. His first competitive race was an Automobile Racing Club of America (ARCA) event at Daytona in 1979. Kyle drove one of his father's cast-off

NASCAR DIECAST AND MODEL CARS

Mattel's Hot Wheels line produced these three 1/24th-scale cars to commemorate 50 years of Pettys in racing. This paint scheme was used on only one occasion—over the Brickyard weekend in 1999.

The Franklin Mint produces a series of four 1/24th-scale Petty cars that include this 1970 Plymouth Superbird and the King's 1967 GTX to commemorate his record season of 27 victories, 10 of which were in a row.

PETTY ENTERPRISES

Dodge Magnums to an impressive victory, giving his story a fairy-tale beginning.

Kyle Petty hasn't reached the heights of either Lee or Richard's accomplishments in racing, but he has nonetheless established himself as one of the most respected drivers in NASCAR Winston Cup racing. This second-generation driver has driven for the Wood Brothers and Team Sabco, and most recently has returned to the family operation to drive the No. 44 Hot Wheels Pontiac. Kyle's career stats show eight career WC victories and over $12 million in winnings.

Adam Petty

Adam Petty, son of Kyle and Patti, upheld the family reputation on the race track in fine style when he was only 18 years old. After many years competing in go-karts and legend cars, the fourth-generation Petty racer spent a year in the highly competitive American Speed Association (ASA) where he won two poles and recorded his first professional victory at Odessa, Missouri. In 1998, in one of his first superspeedway races, Adam won the ARCA event at Lowe's Motor Speedway in Charlotte, North Carolina. Adam quickly moved up to compete in the NASCAR BGN series with occasional appearances in selected Craftsman Truck races.

In a single-car accident during qualifying at New Hampshire Speedway on May 12, 2000, Adam was killed instantly when his race car plowed into the third turn wall. He was the first fourth-generation athlete in professional sports. While we were still celebrating Adam's entry into professional stock car racing, all of us mourned this numbing loss with the Petty family. Adam died five weeks after his great-grandfather, Lee, passed away.

Family Operation

The first 50 years for the Petty clan have been fruitful. Lee Petty won 54 races, and Richard won 200 races. Jim Paschal drove Petty-built cars to 8 wins, and Marvin Panch had 1 win. Pete Hamilton won 3 times in a Petty race car, including the 1970 Daytona 500. Buddy Baker recorded 2 wins while driving for the Pettys. Jimmy Hensley has 2 wins, as do Bobby Hamilton and John Andretti. The total of over 270 NASCAR victories by Petty race cars is a phenomenal record. The team also has a record 10 championships and has won millions of dollars of prize money in the last half century.

A youthful Kyle Petty prepares to take to the Bristol Speedway high banks for practice in April 1981.

Lee Petty models are pretty scarce. Shown here are three vehicles from Racing Champions that include both his 1953 Dodge, and his 1955 Chrysler in 1/64th scale, as well as Lee's 1950 Plymouth business coupe in 1/24th scale.

John Andretti

Since Richard Petty's retirement from the driver's seat after the 1992 season, a number of skilled racers have operated the controls of the famous No. 43 Pontiac including Wally Dallenbach Jr. and Bobby Hamilton. John Andretti, nephew of the legendary Mario Andretti, appears to have found a home at Petty Enterprises and currently drives for the acknowledged "king" of stock car racing. In the past, Andretti has driven for Billy Hagan, Michael Kranefuss, and Cale Yarborough. Andretti's first win came in Yarborough's No. 98 RCA Ford in 1997. In 1998, Andretti had his best showing for Petty Enterprises with an 11th-place finish in championship points. Andretti won at Martinsville for the team in 1999.

NASCAR DIECAST AND MODEL CARS

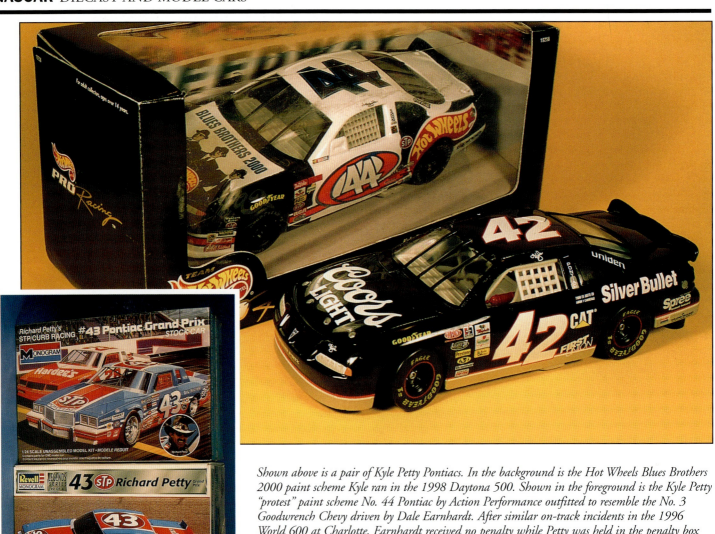

Shown above is a pair of Kyle Petty Pontiacs. In the background is the Hot Wheels Blues Brothers 2000 paint scheme Kyle ran in the 1998 Daytona 500. Shown in the foreground is the Kyle Petty "protest" paint scheme No. 44 Pontiac by Action Performance outfitted to resemble the No. 3 Goodwrench Chevy driven by Dale Earnhardt. After similar on-track incidents in the 1996 World 600 at Charlotte, Earnhardt received no penalty while Petty was held in the penalty box for seven laps. In protest of the Charlotte incident, Team Sabco showed up the following week at Dover for the Miller 500 with this distinctive livery. It was team owner Felix Sabates' contention that NASCAR was playing favorites.

Collectible Richard Petty items include this pair of STP Pontiac Grand Prix plastic kits. Shown here is the 1985 version (No. 2722) and the 1984 200th victory race car (No. 3151).

PETTY ENTERPRISES

Ertl was one of the first manufacturers to tap into the NASCAR diecast market with these two items. Many credit this Ertl 1980 STP Chevy Caprice as being arguably the first 1/24th-scale Petty collectible. In the foreground is an Ertl 1981 STP Buick from their Pull-Back series.

Above is a trio of Petty No. 43 Pontiacs in 1/24th scale. The model on the left is the Racing Champions STP Pontiac that was driven by John Andretti in the 1999 Pepsi 400. A sweeping fire brought many things to a halt in central Florida. The situation caused NASCAR to cancel the July event and reschedule it for the fall. The script on the hood thanks the heroic firefighters. The model in the center, manufactured by Action Performance, depicts the STP 25th anniversary paint scheme of Petty driver Bobby Hamilton's car in 1996. The model on the right is the Racing Champions French's/Black Flag BGN Pontiac that was driven by Rodney Combs for Richard Petty in 1994. Note the two distinctly unique paint schemes on either side of the car's centerline. This livery was run at Daytona that year for the car's first competitive outing. The French's/Black Flag Pontiac is a bank. The Anniversary No. 43 is not a bank, but has black windows, as this denotes the second production run.

39

NASCAR DIECAST AND MODEL CARS

Team Caliber produced this pair of 1/24th-scale Sprint Chevrolets that were driven by the late Adam Petty. On the left is Adam's 2000 WC ride, and on the right is his 1999 Busch series race car.

Steve Grissom

Rich Bickle was selected to drive the Petty CTS entry in the series' first season. Jimmy Hensley then drove the Dodge Ram truck for Richard Petty in the NASCAR CTS through the 1999 season. Hensley, with considerable experience in both the Busch and WC series, was runner-up in points for the Grand National championship twice and was voted NASCAR Rookie-of-the-Year in Winston Cup in 1992. Hensley's first CTS win gave Richard Petty his first victory as a team owner. His second win for the Petty team came at Martinsville in 1999. Steve Grissom piloted the red No. 43 CTS Dodge during the 2000 season. Steve has 11 BGN career victories, and he won the series championship in 1993.

Introduction to Collectibles

Petty racing merchandise and collectibles continue to be very popular with race fans and the general public. This is especially true for Richard Petty, who appears to be as popular or more so in retirement than when he was an active participant. With one of the most recognized names in motorsports, the varieties of Petty paraphernalia virtually boggle the mind.

PETTY ENTERPRISES

Mike Madlinger built this pair of 1/24th Kyle Petty Hot Wheels Pontiacs. On the left is the special No. 44 Charity Ride paint scheme run at Fanta, California, in 1999. On the right is the Hot Wheels paint scheme from the Phoenix 1997 race to commemorate Kyle's 500th start in WC. Both cars are built from the Revell Pontiac Grand Prix kit. The Charity Ride decals are by JustWantToBuild-Models (JWTBM). The 500th start decals are by SLIXX.

Many model kits of Petty race cars have been produced over the last few decades. Virtually every major American model car kit manufacturer (AMT, Revell-Monogram, Jo-han, MPC) at one time or another have produced something bearing the numbers 43, 42, and 44. There are also companies, including Starter and Renaissance, who make 1/43rd-scale kits. Soon, a 1/24th-scale replica of the No. 43 Dodge Ram truck from the 2000 CTS, driven by Steve Grissom, is now available in a plastic kit from Revell-Monogram. If the Petty family and Petty Enterprises manage to endure for another 50 years in racing, we can only ponder the countless collectible items that will be available in the future.

The late Tim Richmond was expected to deliver Hendrick Motorsports' first WC title at the wheel of the No. 25 Folgers Chevrolet.

Two-time NASCAR champion Terry Labonte (left) visits with Richard Petty's cousin and former crew chief Dale Inman (right).

Three-time WC champion Darrell Waltrip drove the Tide No. 5 for Hendrick Motorsports. Waltrip is shown here buckling up in the No. 11 Mountain Dew Buick that he drove to back-to-back championships in 1981 and 1982.

Benny Parsons briefly took over the No. 25 Folgers ride after Tim Richmond's illness in 1987.

5

Hendrick Motorsports

Rick Hendrick is the founder of Hendrick Management Corporation, which controls 84 automotive and truck dealerships in 65 locations and ranks as one of the largest auto retailers in the United States. The company employs 4,500 workers and has annual revenues exceeding $2 billion. Hendrick bought his first auto dealership at age 23 in Bennettsville, South Carolina, and became the youngest Chevrolet dealer in the country. He started as the used car cleanup guy at the dealership while he was in high school and worked his way up to become franchise owner.

Hendrick is the founder of Hendrick Motorsports, which fields three NASCAR Winston Cup (WC) teams. The operation began in 1984, and Hendrick Motorsports race cars have won more than 80 events, including numerous victories in Winston Cup, Busch Grand National (GN), and International Motor Sports Association (IMSA). Jeff Gordon and Terry Labonte, combined, won four consecutive WC championships from 1995 through the 1998 season. Three titles belong to Gordon and one is Labonte's.

Hendrick Motorsports has employed a plethora of extremely talented stock car drivers since the beginning in 1984. That first venture into WC competition was with the No. 5 Chevrolet Monte Carlo with Jeffery Bodine behind the wheel. While the oldest of the three brothers piloted a Hendrick car, the team's first victory came at the Martinsville speedway in Virginia. During Bodine's tenure, Hendrick revelled in his team winning the Daytona 500 for the first time in 1986. Hendrick fielded a second team when country singer T. G. Sheppard brought Rick together with a contact at Procter & Gamble in Cincinnati, Ohio. Hendrick teamed veteran crew chief, Harry Hyde, with newcomer Tim Richmond and the fun began. We will never know what great accomplishment might have come from the Richmond/Hyde duo because the Ohio-born Richmond died of complications of AIDS in 1989.

Ken Schrader took over the Folgers machine for Hendrick Motorsports in 1988. The Procter & Gamble product livery ran out in 1989 and was replaced by American Tobacco's Kodiak brand.

On his way to becoming an independent owner/driver, Darrell Waltrip made a brief stop at Hendrick Motorsports in 1987. Waltrip secured his old No. 17 car from struggling independent Roger Hamby and struck a deal with P&G's Tide soap brand. This second team was also very successful in rewarding Hendrick with many victories, including another Daytona 500 victory by Waltrip in 1989. The one goal that continued to elude Hendrick was a WC championship trophy.

When Waltrip left to form his own team in 1991, he took along the No. 17 and negotiated a sponsorship deal with Western Auto and their national chain of automotive parts stores. Hendrick retained the Tide sponsorship and signed Ricky Rudd to drive the No. 5 car, which had been vacated by Jeff Bodine. Rudd did not disappoint as he was a constant threat at nearly every event. In 1991 Rudd came very close to delivering the big prize to the Hendrick stable as he finished in the runner-up position in the championship battle with eventual season champ Dale Earnhardt.

Hendrick succeeded in hiring 1973 champion Benny Parsons away from Junie Dunlevy to pilot the Folgers No. 25 Chevy. Parsons was energized by the move and front-line equipment, and nearly won the 1987 Daytona 500.

Rudd replaced Bodine in the No. 5 car for the 1990 season. The Levi Garrett sponsorship was replaced by Tide laundry detergent as primary sponsor. Schrader and Rudd continued to play their skills for Hendrick and won their share of races on the highly competitive stock car circuit.

NASCAR DIECAST AND MODEL CARS

Far left: Jeff Gordon has given Rick Hendrick three WC championships so far.

Middle: Kenny Schrader drove the No. 25 car for Rick Hendrick until he left to drive the No. 33 Skoal Chevy.

Far right: Jerry Nadeau delivered a victory in his first season with Hendrick Motorsports.

In 1993, a young Indiana race driver, fresh from great success on the Midwest's short tracks and open-wheel competition, was vying for a spot in the BNG series. Jeff Gordon would have the kind of success with Hendrick Motorsports that Hollywood movie scripts are made of. Hendrick teamed Gordon with Ray Evernham along with Chevrolet race cars and Dupont Paint Finishes as major sponsor. This combination worked like a well-oiled machine and dominated the series through the late 1990s.

Near the end of the 1999 season, Hendrick Motorsports announced that Jerry Nadeau, a Connecticut native and experienced sports car racer, would be their choice to drive the No. 25 Monte Carlo with home builder Michael Holigan as primary sponsor. Jack Sprague, driver of the Quaker State/GMAC Chevrolet in the Craftsman Truck Series (CTS), gave Hendrick Motorsports its first CTS title in 1996. Sprague won the championship again in 1999.

Jeff Gordon

Rick Hendrick had enjoyed some measure of success with a variety of talented drivers before Jeff Gordon came along. Hendrick was impressed with the raw talent Gordon displayed on the race track. Technically Gordon was not under contract to Bill Davis Racing or Ford Motor Company, and Hendrick succeeded in spiriting young Gordon away from the blue oval and quickly signed him to a driving contract in late 1992. Twenty-two-year-old Gordon competed in his very first WC race in 1992 at the Hooters 500 in Atlanta, Georgia.

During the 1993 season, Gordon destroyed a dozen race cars in the season's first 13 events, but Hendrick was determined that Gordon was his ticket to the top. Gordon and Evernham finally got into their rhythm, and by the end of the season, they had risen to the 14th position in points with seven top-five finishes. The "dynamic duo" carried that momentum over into the new season and earned the respect of fans, competitors, and the media by winning two high-visibility events on the schedule—the Coca-Cola 600 at Charlotte and the very first Brickyard 400 at Indianapolis Motor Speedway.

When the 1995 season began, the Chevrolet teams were sporting new sheet metal in the form of a redesigned and more aerodynamic shape that marked the return of the storied Monte Carlo name to stock car racing. Gordon rocketed to seven wins and the first of his three championships. It had taken Hendrick millions of dollars and many lifetimes of patience and endurance, but he could finally celebrate his first NASCAR WC title after 11 years as a team owner.

The 1996 season came down to an intramural match between teammates. When the smoke cleared at season's end, Gordon and Terry Labonte finished first and second in the title chase. Labonte had managed to hold off Gordon down the home stretch and record his second career championship title by a slim 37 points.

To christen the 1997 season, the three Hendrick teammates (Gordon, Labonte, and new addition Ricky Craven) swept the first three places in the season's premier event: the Daytona 500. When the chase ended, Gordon had prevailed in the closest three-way battle for the WC championship in NASCAR history. Just 14 points separated Gordon from second-place Dale Jarrett, and 29 points behind was Mark Martin in third place. Gordon went on to lead the series with 10 victories, and was well on his way to another title.

If the Dupont-sponsored team's past feats weren't enough, 1998 was the same stuff and more. Gordon pulled off some of the most unbelievable comebacks seen in racing circles in decades. Evernham and Gordon combined to break out to a series-record 13 victories. The No. 24 team recorded their second straight title and third championship title in four tries.

For 1999, it appeared the die was firmly set as Gordon and company won their second Daytona 500. As the new season labored on, the rumor mill was full of talk of friction and disharmony within the confines of the No. 24 Hendrick team. Finally, in late September, the media pressure burst the bubble of silence, and Evernham announced his departure from the Hendrick operation.

The unbelievable consistency that was at the heart of the 24 team's success collapsed. There were nine finishes outside

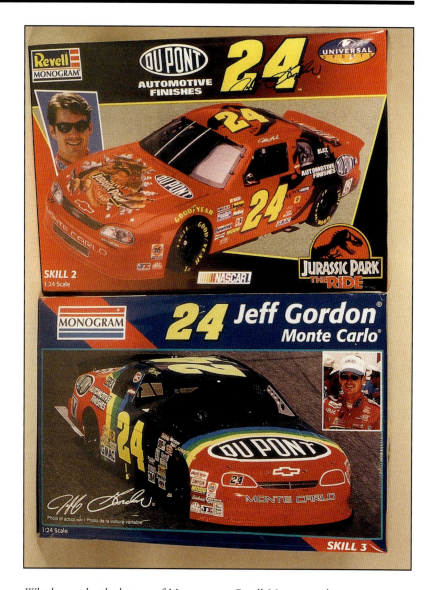

Whether under the banner of Monogram or Revell-Monogram, here are two examples of collectible 1/24th-scale glue kits of the No. 24 Dupont Chevrolet. On the top is the 1997 Jurassic Park version, and on the bottom is the 1996 version (Kit No. 2476).

the top ten. There were seven DNFs that spelled disaster. With new crew chief Brian Whitesell on board, the Dupont team quickly recorded two wins in a row at Martinsville and Charlotte, but it was too little too late.

The next millennium began for the Dupont No. 24 team with a new crew, a redesigned race car (2000 Monte Carlo), a new crew chief, and a new attitude. Robbie Loomis, a seasoned crew chief for the Petty No. 43 team, was wooed over to Hendrick in an attempt to rekindle the magic of 1993 through 1998. The team recorded three victories in 2000, and a 10th-place finish in points in the championship chase.

Terry Labonte

Today, most race fans associate Terry Labonte with Hendrick Motorsports, Kellogg's, the No. 5, and Chevrolets. The senior Labonte, like so many of today's top racers, started off in open-wheel race cars. Terry began his racing career by touring the country running quarter-midgets with the family team. The Labontes cut their racing teeth in this highly competitive type of race car for youngsters in the mid-1960s.

Almost 15 years after gaining experience in other feeder series, Terry made his first appearance in NASCAR Winston Cup in 1978 in a Buick Regal. It was a precursor of the great things to come as Texas Terry finished a strong fourth in the 1978 Southern 500 at Darlington, South Carolina. Terry must have taken a liking to the old "Lady in Black" as his first major stock car victory came at Darlington, and he won there again in the Labor Day–classic Southern 500 on his 58th career start.

Terry Labonte caught the eye of owner/racer Billy Hagan who quickly put Labonte in the seat of his No. 44 race car. First with Budweiser sponsorship and then with the backing of Piedmont Airlines (now part of US Airways), Terry carried the Hagan team to fame and fortune. At the top of his healthy list of accomplishments is winning the 1984 WC championship for Hagan and company. Never able to repeat that level of success again, Labonte left Hagan in 1993 for the Junior Johnson organization to drive Chevrolet Monte Carlos and Ford Thunderbirds sponsored by Budweiser. Terry pushed the No. 11 to many victories, but never was able to be a factor in the big hunt for a nation-

This Hasbro Garage Scene piece features a 1/43rd-scale 1999 No. 24 Dupont Monte Carlo and figures of Jeff Gordon and Ray Evernham.

al championship.

In 1994, Terry found a welcome home with Hendrick Motorsports and was assigned to the driver's seat for the No. 5 Chevrolet Monte Carlo. Labonte succeeded in bringing Kellogg's to accompany him to his new location. That first year Labonte piloted the No. 5 Kellogg's to a seventh place in the final points standings for the WC title with 14 top-ten finishes. His three victories at Richmond, Phoenix, and North Wilkesboro were a personal single-season best for the Texas native..

The No. 5 team headed by Labonte and crew chief Gary DeHart continued to gel with time. The fruits of their combined labors culminated in winning the 1996 NASCAR Winston Cup for Rick Hendrick. This feat marked the first time in series history that one driver had such a span of years between championships. It was also the second title in a row for Hendrick as Labonte squeaked past teammate Jeff Gordon by a scant 37 points.

Labonte's other major achievements came in mid-April 1996. He equaled and surpassed the long-standing record of consecutive starts by Richard Petty, who was the previous all-time NASCAR record holder for consecutive starts. Terry tied the record at North Wilkesboro for his 513th start on April 14, and broke the record for his 514th at Martinsville

HENDRICK MOTORSPORTS

Inset: Shown here is the Monogram 1/24th-scale Tide No. 17 MC Aerocoupe. In the background is the unbuilt kit (No. 2755). Mike Madlinger built this replica of Waltrip's 1989 Daytona 500–winning version by using the Monogram kit and aftermarket decals.

Mike Madlinger built this pair of No. 17 Tide rides. In the foreground is Darrell Waltrip's 1989 Daytona-winning Monte Carlo. In the background is Waltrip's 1990 Lumina, which was built from a Monogram Days of Thunder *kit and aftermarket decals.*

the next weekend. Due to an injury as the result of a crash during the July 2000 Pepsi 400 at Daytona, Labonte's record ended. Persistent medical complications as an aftermath of the crash plagued him. He withdrew from the next few events and finally returned full-strength at Bristol, Tennessee. Labonte's record ended at 655 consecutive starts.

The No. 25 Car
Rick Hendrick realized early on there was an advantage in having more than a single-team effort chasing the coveted WC championship prize. It was thought that pooling resources and technical data from more than one team would allow success to come quickly at less cost.

Tim Richmond
Rick Hendrick worked some magic of his own to bring together the unlikely duo of Ohio-born upstart Tim Richmond with legendary crew chief (the late) Harry Hyde. Richmond had open-wheel experience and was originally

NASCAR DIECAST AND MODEL CARS

Ricky Craven briefly drove the No. 25 car with Budweiser sponsorship. Shown here is a Revell Select Louie the Lizard in 1/24th scale. Next is a Revell Collection in 1/43rd scale and a Racing Champions in 1/144th scale. Since the small scale is supposedly aimed at children, no reference to the primary sponsor, Budweiser, appears on the model.

Benny Parsons took over the No. 25 Folgers ride and used a new number, 35. The author built the replica shown here in the background by using the Monogram kit and aftermarket numbers. Wayne Moyer built the Starter Folgers No. 25 in the foreground.

HENDRICK MOTORSPORTS

This is the Revell Collection No. 25 Coast Guard Bank Set, which features a 1/24th-scale diecast bank and a 1/64th-scale model as part of the two-piece package.

focused on a career in Indy car racing. His short stint there rewarded Richmond with the 1980 rookie title in that year's 500-miler.

Harry Hyde at first had little interest in teaming up with the brash youngster. Hendrick managed somehow to spark the creative juices and a willingness in the old warhorse. Hyde built the race cars and was able to surround himself with the top young talent of the day. The one obstacle that seemed insurmountable at first was getting the veteran and the greenhorn to cooperate and get along. However, the two buried their differences and found their stride. The result was a very cohesive and competitive operation that brought numerous victories and much glory and fame to the Hendrick operation.

Richmond's last year racing for Hendrick was in 1987. We will never know what other great accomplishments might have come from this unlikely motorsports marriage. Tim Richmond had superstar written all over him, but the young buckeye died of complications of AIDS in 1989. The origins of this real-life story found their way into the script for the movie *Days of Thunder*.

Benny Parsons

Rick Hendrick succeeded in hiring 1973 WC champion Benny Parsons away from Junie Dunlevy to pilot the Folgers No. 25 Chevy for the 1987 season. Parsons was energized by the move into front-line equipment. He nearly won the 1988 Daytona 500, and finished a close second to Bill Elliott.

Ken Schrader

Starting with the 1988 season, Ken Schrader took over the Folgers machine for Hendrick Motorsports. The Procter & Gamble livery ran out in 1989 and was replaced by American Tobacco's Kodiak brand. Schrader drove for Hendrick from 1988 through 1996, and only scored four victories during that time. Schrader left Hendrick to drive the No. 33 Skoal Chevy for Andy Petree Racing.

Ricky Craven

When Schrader left the Hendrick Motorsports operation after a lackluster 1996 season, Busch North standout Ricky Craven took over the No. 25 Chevy. The Anheuser-Busch beer brand Budweiser came on board as the primary sponsor. The Maine native first competed in BGN with a degree of success before moving to WC in 1995.

Craven possessed an impressive resume from his years in the NASCAR Busch North series, and started off with great promise, being part of the 1-2-3 sweep by the Hendrick team in the 1998 Daytona 500. Soon after the sweep, the No. 25 Bud Chevy team struggled. Craven suffered a concussion in a practice accident and was sidelined for a while. When Craven returned to competition, he suffered a second serious crash. Hendrick Motorsports made the decision to replace Craven and a string of other drivers, including Randy LaJoie and Wally Dallenbach Jr.

Jerry Nadeau

Jerry Nadeau, a Connecticut native and experienced sports car racer, got the nod to join the team before the beginning of the 2000 season. Near the end of the 1999 season, Hendrick Motorsports announced that Nadeau would be their choice to drive the No. 25 Monte Carlo with home builder Michael Holigan as the primary sponsor.

Nadeau seemed to click with his new team early in the season. A number of excellent runs toward midseason gave an early indication that the new No. 25 team was a serious

NASCAR DIECAST AND MODEL CARS

Shown on top is a Testors 1998 Kellogg's No. 5 in prepainted kit form. On the bottom is a 2000 Racing Champions (RC) prepainted kit of the No. 5. Both items are made by RC. The Testor's piece was sold under that name before RC acquired Ertl/AMT.

threat to record a victory in 2000. That hypothesis proved to be quite accurate, even though it took the MH2 team until the final event of the season to blossom. In the season finale at Atlanta, Nadeau started alongside fellow teammate Jeff Gordon at the green flag. Five laps later, Nadeau took the lead. Running out front or near the front all afternoon, it was no surprise when Nadeau was able to out-duel seven-time champ Dale Earnhardt Sr. in the closing laps for his first NASCAR WC win.

The history of the No. 25 team is one of near-greatness and star-crossed efforts. Since the early successes of the late Tim Richmond, the Hendrick Motorsports No. 25 Chevrolet has never equaled the promise forecast in the mid-1980s. The combination at Hendrick Motorsports for the 2001 season keeps driver Nadeau and his team intact and combines them with new primary sponsor Delphi-UAW. There's every indication that the No. 25 team will be a contender in the future.

Introduction to Collectibles

Stock car collectibles for this team range from plastic model kits of the 1986 Folgers No. 25 Monte Carlo driven by the late Tim Richmond and virtually every race car driven by Jeff Gordon, to numerous diecast models of the Kellogg's No. 5 Chevy driven by Terry Labonte. Darrell Waltrip's 1987 Tide No. 17 Chevy was immortalized in both 1/43rd scale by the French company Starter and 1/24th scale by Revell-Monogram. Both of these items are unassembled model kits. The smaller one is made of resin while the R-M kit is molded in polystyrene plastic.

With the increased interest in collecting diecast race cars in the last few years, the number of new plastic kit releases has declined sharply. As an example, at one time, each new season's changes in sponsors and paint schemes was reflected in model kit form. To fill this void, aftermarket decal manufacturers, such as Fred Cady Design and SLIXX, offer a wide variety of Hendrick race car markings that allow the kit builder to build rather than simply collect a specific model.

HENDRICK MOTORSPORTS

For the Terry Labonte fan, here are five Kellogg's No. 5 diecast models in four scales. In the background is a Team Caliber 2000 No. 5, a Revell Collection 1/43rd-scale 1998 Tony the Tiger No. 5, a 1999 Hasbro Kellogg's No. 5 in 1/64th-scale, and a pair of 1/144th-scale Racing Champions of the 1997 Kellogg's Chevy.

This is a pair of Revell Collection 1997 Tony the Tiger diecast Chevys that were driven by Terry Labonte. In the background is a 1/24th-scale version, and in the foreground is a 1/43rd-scale of the same car.

51

Seven-time NASCAR champ Dale Earnhardt recorded his first WC victory at Bristol Motor Speedway in April 1979.

6

Richard Childress Racing/Dale Earnhardt Inc.

Today, Richard Childress is one of the most successful team owners in the history of NASCAR racing. Since making the transition from driver to team owner in 1981, Richard Childress Racing (RCR) has been party to six of Dale Earnhardt's seven Winston Cup (WC) championships, and one Craftsman Truck Series (CTS) championship by Mike Skinner.

It hasn't always been a milk-and-honey existence for Childress. He labored at competing in major-league stock car racing for 12 years. For Childress to survive, it took a great deal of calculation, shrewdness, and resourceful ability to get the most out of the finances, equipment, and opportunities he was dealt.

In 1980, when the challenges seemed insurmountable, Childress sought the advice of close friend and former-driver-turned-team-owner Junior Johnson. Johnson's advice to Childress was to take the lessons and skills learned in the school of hard knocks and switch roles. Childress has never regretted taking Johnson's advice to heart.

After winning Rookie-of-the-Year in 1979 and the 1980 WC championship, Dale Earnhardt accepted the driving duties for RCR for the 1981 season. Earnhardt managed only two top-fives during that first season with RCR. Earnhardt accepted an offer to drive Bud Moore's No. 15 Ford Thunderbird for 1982. Meanwhile, Childress provided an opportunity for a young Virginia driver named Ricky Rudd. The two teamed for the 1982 and 1983 seasons. Driving the Piedmont Airlines No. 3 Chevy, Rudd scored his first WC victory in 1982, and it was also the first win for Childress as a car owner. Rudd followed this up with two wins for RCR in 1983.

For the 1984 season, Moore and Childress pulled a driver swap which reunited Dale Earnhardt with RCR. Of the six championship seasons that Earnhardt drove for RCR, the team won 39 races which included nearly every event except for the Daytona 500. That win didn't come until 1998 during a non-championship season.

In 1997, RCR became one of the last major operations to add a second team. Lowe's Home Improvements' Larry McReynolds and Mike Skinner were teamed to campaign the No. 31 Chevys. For the 2001 NASCAR season, RCR rolled out the Goodwrench No. 3 for Dale Earnhardt Sr. once again. Earnhardt's tragic death during the final lap of the Daytona 500 caused Childress to elevate rookie Kevin Harvick to the seat of the now-renumbered No. 29 Goodwrench Chevy. Mike Skinner will continue in the the No. 31 Lowe's Chevy for 2001. RCR has also provided a pair of Busch Grand National (BGN) Chevrolets for Mike Dillon and Kevin Harvick.

Dale Earnhardt

Throughout his illustrious career, race fans have either loved or hated Dale Earnhardt. There are no neutral fans when it comes to the "Intimidator." His aggressive, bump-and-run, "it-was-just-a-racing-accident" driving style has earned him millions of loyal fans. In contrast, those same attributes got him loads of loud boos and catcalls from many quarters.

The son of the late racing standout Ralph Earnhardt, Dale Sr. began his NASCAR Winston Cup racing career in 1975 when Ed Negre gave him his big break. The second-generation driver competed in his first NASCAR WC race, and piloted the No. 8 1974 Dodge Charger. That exposure led to Californian Rod Osterland hiring Earnhardt to drive his No. 2 Chevys and Oldsmobiles full-time for the 1979 season.

The Osterland team provided Earnhardt with solid equipment. The Kannapolis, North Carolina, native scored

53

NASCAR DIECAST AND MODEL CARS

Shown here is Mike Skinner (right) talking to former DEI driver Ron Hornaday at Sears Point, California in 1998.

Steve Park captured his first career WC victory at Watkins Glen in 2000.

Dale Earnhardt Jr. just missed winning the coveted Rookie-of-the-Year title in 2000

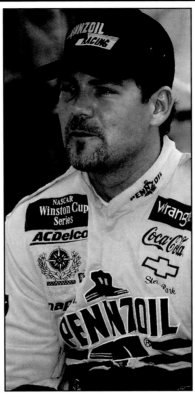

his first career win and the Rookie-of-the-Year title that first season. The momentum obviously carried over into the next season, and Earnhardt and Osterland again combined for a very competitive year as they beat out the Junior Johnson and Cale Yarborough duo for the 1980 Winston Cup championship title.

When Osterland closed up shop and went home to California, Earnhardt accepted the driving duties at RCR. The RCR No. 2 Wrangler Pontiac team had a lackluster season. Earnhardt managed only two top-fives during his first season with Childress. Earnhardt carried the yellow-and-blue Wrangler colors with him as he drove Bud Moore's Fords for most of the 1982–1983 season. He managed just three wins for the veteran car owner. During this period, Childress employed newcomer Ricky Rudd to drive his Piedmont Chevys, and the team got the first win for both car owner and driver in 1983.

For the 1984 season, Moore and Childress pulled a driver swap which reunited Earnhardt with the RCR team. Wrangler followed Earnhardt back to the Childress operation as primary sponsor. Of the six championship seasons that Earnhardt drove for RCR, the team won 39 races, which included nearly every event except for the Daytona 500. That win finally came after 19 tries in 1998. In 2000, Dale Sr. came close to winning his eighth WC title. Throughout his WC career, Earnhardt won the Daytona 500 only twice with 13 top-fives, 24 top-tens, and 3 second-place finishes.

Just shy of age 50, Dale Earnhardt Sr. had a long list of career accomplishments. His seven championships match those of Richard Petty. Earnhardt's 76 victories put him at

RICHARD CHILDRESS RACING/DALE EARNHARDT INC.

This Monogram No. 3 Wrangler Combo kit proved to be one of the most popular NASCAR double kits produced by this manufacturer.

This collection of five 1/64th-scale diecast cars is an excellent chronicle of Dale Earnhardt's illustrious career. In the background are three Winner's Circle items depicting the 1979, 1986, and 2000 seasons. In the foreground is an Ertl 1982 Wrangler T-Bird and a Revell Collection No. 3 honoring the 1996 Olympics car that was driven by Earnhardt in the Winston that year.

the top of the list of active drivers of the 2001 season. Earnhardt has four International Race of Champions (IROC) titles to his credit. He is one of the sport's all-time leading money winners.

At the beginning of the 2001 NASCAR racing season, the unthinkable happened. On the last lap of the Daytona 500, the series' biggest race, Dale Earnhardt Sr. was killed instantly as his familiar black No. 3 slammed into the wall head-on. Ironically, it was Dale Earnhardt, Inc.'s (DEI) two drivers Michael Waltrip and Dale, Jr. who finished 1-2 in the big event. It was Waltrip's first WC victory after nearly 500 starts.

Earnhardt, Sr. had always enjoyed great success at the legendary Florida race track. Even though he had won a number of support events over the years, it wasn't until 1998 that Dale Sr. recorded his first and only victory in the Daytona 500.

The establishment of DEI put Dale Sr. in the position of team owner. Its home, a 108,000-square-foot facility in Mooresville, North Carolina, is an absolute state-of-the-art operation. The racing plant houses an abundance of office, garage, and museum space under one roof.

DEI began fielding Busch cars for drivers, including Jeff Green and Steve Park. In 1997, Dale Earnhardt Jr. took over the No. 3 Delco Chevy. Running the BGN circuit full-time, the third-generation driver won back-to-back titles for DEI in 1998 and 1999. Steve Park was added to the roster in the No. 1 Pennzoil Chevrolet Monte Carlo in 1998 and remains a solid competitor. The DEI team also competed in the CTS from the inaugural season of 1995 through 1999. During

NASCAR DIECAST AND MODEL CARS

This is a trio of Starter 1/43rd-scale resin kits built by Wayne Moyer. From left to right is a 1987 Wrangler Chevy, 1988 Goodwrench Monte Carlo, and 1991 Goodwrench Chevrolet Lumina.

that period, Californian Ron Hornaday won the title in 1996 and 1998 to compile 25 victories and remains the all-time leader in the series.

DEI continues to campaign the No. 8 Budweiser Chevy for Dale, Jr. and the No. 1 Pennzoil Monte Carlo for Steve Park in 2001. The BGN effort was shelved at the end of the 2000 season in order to add a third WC team. Michael Waltrip signed on to drive the No. 15 NAPA Chevy and won the Daytona 500 in his first outing for the team.

Mike Skinner

Mike Skinner grew up in Susanville, California. He began honing his racing skills on the dirt tracks of northern California and western Nevada over 20 years ago. Skinner enjoyed considerable success in open-competition late-model stock cars, enough so that he decided to pursue his dreams elsewhere. After he relocated to North Carolina, Skinner picked up where he left off on the local short tracks around the Charlotte area.

When NASCAR established the new CTS in 1995, RCR committed to the new league. Skinner had caught the attention of Childress who hired him to drive the Goodwrench No. 3 Chevy C-1500. Skinner rewarded his new owner by winning the first race he competed in, and winning the CTS title in 1995 with 10 poles, 17 top fives, 18 top tens, and 8 victories. He ran CTS full-time the next year taking 5 poles and recording a total of 16 career victories before he moved up to WC competition.

Richard Childress decided to expand his RCR to a two-car operation for 1997. Skinner was selected to drive the Lowe's Home Improvement No. 31 Chevy. Recapping that initial season, he won the pole for both Daytona events (Daytona 500 and Pepsi 400, the first rookie to do so) and was selected the 1997 WC Rookie-of-the-Year.

RICHARD CHILDRESS RACING/DALE EARNHARDT INC.

Here is a pair of 1/24th-scale Action Performance Goodwrench No. 3 Chevy Monte Carlos that were modeled after the vehicle driven by Dale Earnhardt in the Winston invitational race at Lowe's Motor Speedway in Charlotte, North Carolina. On the left is the paint scheme commemorating the 1996 Olympics in Atlanta, and on the right is the special silver paint scheme used in the 1997 WC celebrating Winston's 25 years with NASCAR racing.

A pair of 1/24th-scale Action Performance Goodwrench Chevy Monte Carlos are outfitted in special paint schemes. On the left is the Wheaties cereal brand layout in orange that was used in the 1997 Winston Invitational. On the right is the Peter Max–designed scheme that the Childress team used in the 2000 Winston and World 600 races.

Since entering WC competition in 1997, Skinner has finished 30th, 21st, and 10th in points. During this period, however, he did win two NASCAR non-point exhibition races in Suzuka, Japan. Skinner also has a Daytona 500 125-mile-qualifier victory to his credit.

In 2000, Skinner again managed to not win a points-paying race for yet another season. He had only 1 top five and 11 top-tens to his credit in 2000. In spite of a decided lack of consistency, Skinner still managed a 12th-place finish in WC championship points standings.

The outlook for the 2001 season for Skinner and the No. 31 Chevy team is unsettled at best. Crew chief Larry McReynolds is leaving to work behind the microphone for Fox Sports. Primary sponsor Lowe's will replace the familiar yellow-and-blue paint scheme on the No. 31 Chevy with new colors for one of their ancillary product lines.

Steve Park

Steve Park's considerable driving talents in the NASCAR Modified series were brought to the attention of Dale Earnhardt in 1996. The senior Earnhardt was impressed with what he heard and saw, and put the East Northport, New York, native under contract to drive for DEI. While he competed in the NASCAR Modified series, Park recorded 15 feature wins, 22 poles, and was voted the series' most popular driver in 1995.

In 1997, Park began driving for Earnhardt in the BGN series, where he recorded victories at Nashville, Tennessee; Brooklyn, Michigan; and Richmond, Virginia. His good finish in the points standings plus the three victories helped him to garner the 1997 BGN Rookie-of-the-Year award.

Steve Park graduated to WC for the 1998 season. DEI struck a primary sponsorship deal with petroleum giant

NASCAR DIECAST AND MODEL CARS

Above: *Action Performance produced this 1/24th-scale No. 31 Lowe's duo. On the left is the standard Lowe's layout used for a majority of events in 1998. On the right is the Special Olympics paint treatment intended to be used in the 1998 Winston Invitational race prior to the World 600 at Lowe's Motor Speedway in Charlotte, North Carolina, but the paint scheme was never used during the race.*

So far there are only two No. 31 Lowe's Chevy plastic kits available. The kit on top is the 1997 Revell-Monogram kit (No. 2523), and the 2000 Revell kit (No. 85-2991) is on the bottom.

Pennzoil. Use of the No. 1 car number was purchased from the Leo Jackson team for the new race car.

The battle for 1998 WC rookie honors was expected to be one of the most competitive in many years. It looked to be a friendly rivalry between Ford's Kenny Irwin and Chevrolet's Steve Park, but it would prove to be a short-lived contest. As he made a qualifying attempt for the March race at Atlanta Motor Speedway, Park hit the fourth turn wall and finally careened into the pit wall. Park would be out of action for a good portion of the remainder of the 1998 season. The rookie title went to the late Kenny Irwin almost by default. Park, mended and physically fit, returned to full-time competition in 1999. Although he struggled in the first half of the new season, the team managed some decent finishes and eventually recorded a 14th place in the championship points chase.

For the 2000 season, Park won his first WC race by capturing the demanding road course event at Watkins Glen, New York. Park closed out the 2000 season with 6 top fives and 13 top tens to finish 11th in the season's championship standings.

Dale Earnhardt Jr.

Following in the footsteps of a famous racing father is anything but easy, and with Sr.'s death, the added pressure on Dale Earnhardt Jr. is tremendous. It's a special challenge when you both share the same name. For Dale Earnhardt Jr. there were already certain built-in expectations and a high level of accomplishment that was expected right up front.

Dale Earnhardt Jr. (Junior, as some have come to call him) started racing at the age of 17 in the street-stock division

RICHARD CHILDRESS RACING/DALE EARNHARDT INC.

Below: *Shown here is a set of three No. 1 Pennzoil Monte Carlos driven by Steve Park. The 1/24th-scale piece is by Action Performance and commemorates Park's return to the series at the Brickyard 400 in 1998. The standard paint scheme in the 1/43rd- and 1/64th-scale diecast is from Hasbro's Winner's Circle line.*

Above: *The Revell Collection is responsible for this pair of 1999 Special Olympics No. 31 Chevys in 1/24th and 1/43rd scales.*

at Concord (North Carolina) Speedway. After two seasons, Earnhardt Jr. moved up to compete in the NASCAR Late Model Stock Division. From the beginning, his father encouraged him to develop a knowledge of race car preparation and chassis setup.

By 1997, young Earnhardt (a third-generation driver) had developed a reputation, through his considerable driving skills, on tracks throughout North and South Carolina. Hired to drive for his father's operation, Dale Earnhardt, Inc., Junior took a bold but calculated step.

Dale Jr. joined the Busch series fulltime in 1997. In his first outing, he qualified 7th and finished a respectable 13th at Myrtle Beach, South Carolina. He didn't get to victory lane until April when he won at Texas Motor Speedway. The flood gates opened as Dale Jr. ripped off wins at Dover, Milwaukee, Fontana, Indianapolis, Richmond, and St. Louis.

Dale Jr. swept to his first BGN title over rival Matt Kenseth. For 1998, it was more of the same as Junior got a late start but hit a hot streak and won the championship again over Jeff Green and Matt Kenseth. "Little E" recorded 13 wins in his two seasons in BGN.

After winning back-to-back titles in the BGN series, Dale Earnhardt Jr. was touted as a virtual shoo-in for the 2000 season Rookie-of-the-Year title. At the wheel of the No. 8 Budweiser Chevrolet Monte Carlo, Junior took two early victories, but faded dramatically in the second half of the season, getting beat out for the rookie award by Matt Kenseth. The Earnhardt Jr. stats for 2000 list two wins, three top-fives, five top-tens, and a 16th place in the final WC points standings. The 2001 season for Earnhardt Jr. appears to be "on track," as he will be back at the wheel of the No. 8 Bud Chevy once more.

NASCAR DIECAST AND MODEL CARS

Upper Left: *This is a duo of No. 31 Dale Earnhardt Jr. Chevy Monte Carlos from the 1996 and 1997 seasons. The Gargoyles Sunglasses layout (left) is from the 1997 season. The Mom 'n' Pops No. 31 BGN Monte Carlo was campaigned during the 1996 season. Note the associate sponsor on the flanks of the Mom 'n' Pops–Dale Earnhardt Chevrolet.*

Lower Left: *The Hasbro Winner's Circle Victory Celebration series includes this item made to commemorate Dale Jr.'s 1998 BGN championship. Note that his car owner is also sharing the spotlight.*

RICHARD CHILDRESS RACING/DALE EARNHARDT INC.

Upper Right: *Dale Earnhardt Jr. made his rookie debut in the NASCAR WC series in 2000. He competed in seven selected events in 1999 as prescribed by the series rules, thereby making him fully eligible for the Rookie-of-the-Year title chase in 2000. Shown here on the right is the 2000 U.S. Olympic team markings he ran in the August Bristol event. The replica on the left depicts the standard paint scheme Dale Jr. used in selected 1999 WC events.*

Lower Right: *This trio of No. 3 Delco Monte Carlos depicts Dale Earnhardt Jr.'s 1998 championship-winning race car in three scales. Shown here is a 1/24th-scale Revell Collection, and 1/43rd- and 1/64th-scale cars from Hasbro's Winner's Circle line.*

Introduction to Collectibles

The RCR and DEI operations, although two separate racing facilities, are hard to review separately since the late Dale Earnhardt Sr. was the owner of DEI and was lead driver for RCR. These two teams are presented here as stock car racing's virtual "Siamese twins." The hard connection between the two teams will continue to be Dale Earnhardt Sr. Adding to this symbiotic relationship is the fact that both teams share racing technology and testing data.

RCR/DEI Diecast Models and Plastic Kits

Without debate, diecast models and plastic kits bearing the number 3 will remain among the most popular items in any of the product types or price ranges. Whether it's a 99¢ 1/64th-scale Hot Wheels, a $15 plastic kit, or a $100 premium diecast, Dale Earnhardt collectibles have been hot property and big business for many years now. With his recent death, prices and availability are likely to increase.

There are few examples of a manufacturer without a licensing contract with either RCR or DEI personalities. In most cases, few manufacturers are able to secure an exclusive licensing agreement with these entities to allow for a much broader selection of products.

Over at DEI the situation is quite a bit different. Although there were numerous diecast models and one plastic kit of the No. 30 Pennzoil Pontiac from the Bahari team, this has not been the case since the sponsor moved to the No. 1 car driven by Steve Park. There are selected diecast items, but so far there has not been a single plastic kit issued of the DEI Pennzoil Chevy.

Even with the overwhelming popularity of the Budweiser No. 8 Chevrolet Monte Carlo of Dale Earnhardt Jr., models and kits have been a mixed blessing at best. Because of the "politically correct" attitude toward beer- and tobacco-labeled products, true replicas of Jr.'s race cars exist only in the high-end "adult collectible" market. Low-cost diecast are not available with the correct "Bud" or "Budweiser" livery usually displayed on the hood and quarter panels of the full-size race car. So far, no plastic model kit of the No. 8 Chevy exists. There is talk of such an item being produced under the "adult collectible" label as a predecorated glue-style kit. At the time this book was published, the kit concept has been approved by Chevrolet and DEI. We are all waiting for Anheuser-Busch to make up their minds.

Top left: The late Davey Allison was the 1987 NASCAR Rookie-of-the-Year.

Bottom left: Ernie Irvan drove the Kodak Chevy before taking over the No. 28 car.

Top right: The late Kenny Irwin was an open-wheel standout before he moved on to stock cars.

Bottom right: Dale Jarrett won the WC championship in 1999.

7

Robert Yates Racing

Robert Yates got his big break in racing when he was hired to manage the Holman-Moody air gauge department in 1968. After Ford withdrew from racing, Yates moved on to become the chief engine builder for DiGard Racing. Bobby Allison captured the 1983 NASCAR Winston Cup (WC) championship driving Buick Regals powered by Yates-built small-block GM V-8 engines.

Next, Yates moved to the Harry Ranier team during the mid-1980s. After laboring for the Kentucky coal magnate, Yates found Ranier deeply indebted to him for services rendered. Eventually, Yates inherited the assets of the Ranier operation just in time to prepare a car for the 1987 Daytona 500. Young second-generation rookie Davey Allison was quickly signed to drive the new Yates Ford Thunderbirds.

Robert Yates Racing (RYR) Team History

It was a slow start in 1987 as the Yates No. 28 'Bird arrived in Daytona with no sponsorship. Although they didn't finish this first race together, the No. 28 team had garnered attention enough to soon attract Texaco/Havoline as their major sponsor. During the 1987 season, Davey Allison went on to record two victories (at the time it was a record for rookie drivers). Allison was also a runaway winner in the competition for the NASCAR Rookie-of-the-Year title.

By 1992, Allison had captured the Yates team's first Daytona 500 victory. He was a prime contender for the Winston Cup title that year and finished third behind Alan Kulwicki and Bill Elliott.

A dark year for NASCAR racing and Yates was 1993. Newly-crowned WC champ Alan Kulwicki was killed in a plane crash on April 1, 1993. Later that year, Davey Allison was killed in a helicopter crash while flying into Talladega Speedway to view a practice session. The Yates team finished out the season with a variety of drivers, including Lake Speed.

In 1994 Yates secured the services of Ernie Irvan to drive the No. 28 T-Bird. The team immediately rose to the occasion by shooting to the top of the standings with 5 poles, 11 top fives, 16 top tens, and 3 victories. It was shaping up as a banner year for the Yates operation when disaster struck. Irvan was nearly killed in a practice accident for the June race at Michigan International Speedway (MIS). He recovered and returned to race again for the Robert Yates team late in the 1995 season.

Dale Jarrett left the Joe Gibbs No. 18 team to drive for Yates and the No. 28 Texaco/Havoline Ford. It was a lackluster season filled with frustration for the team and the new driver. Irvan returned to competition in August 1995 in Yates car No. 88. He visited victory lane and won the June race at MIS in 1996, where just two years earlier he had nearly lost his life.

Yates decided on a full-time, two-car operation for the 1996 season. Ernie moved back to the Texaco/Havoline No. 28, while Jarrett teamed with new crew chief Todd Parrott under the Quality Care-Red Carpet Leasing primary sponsorship. The new No. 88 team came together quickly and won the 1996 Daytona 500.

In the intervening years RYR has become a major force in NASCAR racing. Jarrett scored the first WC championship for Yates in the No. 88 Taurus in 1999. He scored a fourth-place finish in points during the 2000 season that was highlighted by his third career Daytona 500 victory. In contrast, the tale of the No. 28 team continued to be star-crossed. After Irvan left to drive the M&M No. 36 Pontiac, open-wheel star Kenny Irwin took the controls for the 1998 season. Irwin struggled through and was selected Rookie-of-the-Year. After two disappointing seasons, Irwin went to work for Team Sabco and lost his life driving the No. 42 Bell South Chevy in the 2000 season. Robert Yates hired Ricky

NASCAR DIECAST AND MODEL CARS

Ricky Rudd took over the No. 28 Taurus for the 2000 season.

The story of the No. 28 team in the modern era actually starts with Hardee's cars. These are a pair of stock cars that were driven by Cale Yarborough. The author built both the 1/24th-scale 1983 Hardee's Monte Carlo on the left from Monogram kit No. 3153 and Starter 1/43rd-scale 1985 Thunderbird pictured on the right.

Rudd to drive the 28 car for 2000. Although the team did not post a victory, they managed a strong showing and finished out the season in fifth place in championship points.

The No. 88 team will sport the colors of the new primary sponsor, United Parcel Service, for the 2001 season. Texaco has teamed again with RYR to sponsor the No. 28 team for the new season. Both drivers are considered serious threats to win the 2001 championship.

Davey Allison

David Carl (Davey) Allison's name is still one of the most recognized in professional motorsports. His meteoric rise to stardom in NASCAR stock car racing was short-lived, but nonetheless impressive.

Allison was rapidly headed for superstardom and came within a whisker of winning the NASCAR WC championship in 1992. He died in July 1993 in a helicopter crash at Talladega that also nearly claimed the life of longtime mentor and family friend Red Farmer, who was a passenger in the helicopter.

For many racing fans, the gut-wrenching emotional pain of the Allison tragedy is still associated with other names—Tim Richmond, Alan Kulwicki, Neil Bonnett, Dale Earnhardt, Adam Petty, and Kenny Irwin. Motorsports, on occasion, demands the ultimate sacrifice from its participants, and acceptance of that is a sobering reality for fans.

Davey's story is just part of the litany of tragedies that befell the entire Allison family. It started with a non-life-threatening crash that ended father Bobby's career at Pocono in 1988. This was followed by the death of Davey's younger brother, Clifford, in a practice accident at Michigan Speedway in 1992, and Davey was killed in a helicopter crash while flying to a practice session at the Alabama track in 1993.

Eventually, the unbearable grief pressured Bobby and his wife, Judy, to divorce. Bobby sold off his NASCAR race team and nearly every other personal possession, and he continues to live his life one day at a time. In 2000, Bobby and Judy Allison were reunited at the funeral of Adam Petty and have since remarried.

ROBERT YATES RACING

Above: *Shown here is Revell's 1/24th-scale kit No. 85-2990 of Davey Allison's 1988 T-Bird. Daryl Huhtala built the model that depicts the car as it raced in the 1988 Daytona 500.*

Left: *Wayne Moyer built this 1987 No. 28 Texaco/Havoline Thunderbird, driven by the late Davey Allison, from a Starter kit. Note the contents of the kit and the body wrapped in bubble pack.*

Davey got his big break in racing when industrialist Harry Ranier hired him to fill the seat in the No. 28 T-Bird vacated by Cale Yarborough. When the team arrived in Daytona for the 1987 500-miler, the race car's flanks were bare. The rookie driver and the rejuvenated Ranier-Lundy team had not been able to catch the eye of a major sponsor, but that would quickly change.

Davey, knowing a good showing in NASCAR's premier event would receive a lot of attention, put his brightly painted Thunderbird on the front row during qualifying. It marked the first time a rookie had accomplished this feat. He followed that up by winning his 125-mile qualifying race. Although Davey dropped out of the 1987 Daytona 500 with mechanical trouble, the exposure caught the attention of petroleum giant Texaco. The Texas-based conglomerate paid handsomely to put their big red star on the hood and Havoline motor oil brand name on the rear fenders of Davey's race car. Davey went on to win two races his first year in WC racing, and captured the coveted NASCAR Rookie-of-the-Year title in the process.

In 1992, Davey won his first Daytona 500 at the wheel of a Robert Yates Ford Thunderbird. It was a good competitive year on the grinding coast-to-coast schedule for the new team as they went on to challenge for the WC title and eventually finish third in the season's points tally. During his eight and a half seasons in WC racing, Davey won 19 races; 15 of them on superspeedways. At the time of his passing, Davey had become a threat to win wherever the series competed.

Today, Davey Allison is still a very popular figure among millions of dedicated stock car racing fans. He is remembered as a fierce competitor and talented superstar, and, as eventual team owner and close friend Robert Yates recalls, "though he was very competitive in a race car, he liked to cut up. He was always in a good mood."

After Davey's untimely passing, the Robert Yates team eventually returned to the series and finished out the season with a number of drivers at the wheel of the No. 28 Thunderbird. This set the stage for another major chapter in this story.

This 1/24th-scale No. 2 Monte Carlo that Ernie Irvan drove during his rookie year was built by the author using a Monogram kit and JNJ decals. Mike Madlinger built the 1991 No. 4 Kodak Chevy that Ernie Irvan drove to victory in the 1991 Daytona 500.

Ernie Irvan

Near the end of the 1993 season, Ernie Irvan was named as the permanent replacement to drive the Texaco/Havoline No. 28 for the late Davey Allison. The decision on the part of Robert Yates was both heavily criticized and greatly praised by those inside and outside the sport. Obviously, the most controversial subject was the crash that involved Allison and Irvan at Atlanta in the final race of the 1992 season. That crash cost Davey the 1992 NASCAR title. Irvan was forced to break his contract with the Morgan-McClure/Kodak No. 4 to accept the high-profile seat in the Yates car.

After bouncing around in midpack or back-marker equipment during the late 1980s, the California native landed the front-runner seat in the Kodak No. 4 Chevrolet in 1991. While aboard the Morgan-McClure machine, Irvan gave the team their first victory at the 1992 Daytona 500. In four seasons with Morgan-McClure, Irvan won 7 races, had a total of 33 top-fives, 51 top-tens, and 9 poles in the bright yellow Chevy. Contrary to the opinions of his detractors, Irvan's performance in the Texaco/Havoline Thunderbird paid quick dividends for the Yates team as he recorded two victories in the final 9 races of the 1993 season.

In 1994, Irvan quickly rose to the challenge as a front-runner for the NASCAR WC championship. However, the events that lay ahead for the California native would reshape his life and racing career forever. Irvan was embroiled in a neck-and-neck points battle with seven-time champ Dale Earnhardt. Irvan had established an early lead, but had slid back into second place behind Earnhardt by 27 points as the series returned to Michigan for the August 21 event. During an early Saturday morning practice session, Irvan's Ford crashed nearly head-on into the turn two concrete retaining wall. The seriously injured driver had to be cut from the mangled race car. Upon examination by the track's medical staff, Irvan was given less than a 10 percent chance of survival.

ROBERT YATES RACING

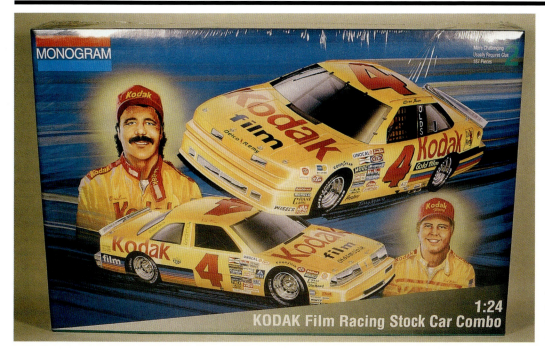

A Kodak Combo double kit No. 6367 from Monogram features the 1991 Kodak Oldsmobile driven by Ernie Irvan.

Irvan survived those first critical hours in an Ann Arbor, Michigan, emergency room. Showing the same tenacity that saw him record 12 series wins before the accident, Irvan beat the odds by overcoming near-fatal head injuries and returned to race once more after considerable therapy. Irvan won on three occasions for the Yates team after his return, including a very emotional win in the Michigan event that nearly took his life.

For the 1998 season, Irvan lost his ride with the Texaco/Havoline No. 28 team. The sponsor had decided to go with a promising young driver named Kenny Irwin who, like three-time champ Jeff Gordon, carried impressive credentials from the Midwest open-wheel ranks.

Irvan would be hired by the MB2 NASCAR team to pilot the No. 36 M&M Pontiac Grand Prix for the new season. During the 1999 season, Irvan suffered more internal and head injuries as the result of grinding practice accidents. During the season, Irvan chose to retire from competition rather than run the risk of losing everything else that was dear to him.

Dale Jarrett

In 1999, Dale Jarrett accomplished what only one other second-generation driver had done before him. Ned and Dale Jarrett are only the second father/son combination to win the NASCAR Winston Cup championship. The first father and son to do so were Lee and Richard Petty.

Dale Jarrett's goal has always been to capture the highest honors of the sport he is so devoted to. From his early years in Busch Grand National (BGN) and Winston Cup (WC), Dale wanted more than anything to follow in his famous father's footsteps. In 1999, Jarrett recorded 4 victories, 24 top fives, and 29 top tens on his way to the WC championship. Only twice in the 1990s was a Ford driver crowned champion.

Even with a name like Jarrett, things never seemed to come easy for young Dale. To get his first shot in late-model

NASCAR DIECAST AND MODEL CARS

This pair of Revell Collection diecast models commemorates the 10-year anniversary of Texaco as sponsor of the No. 28 car. The car on the left is 1/18th scale, and the vehicle on the right is in 1/64th scale.

stock cars, he agreed to raise the money to pay for the car's engine. The one catch to his philanthropic efforts was that he drove the race car!

Jarrett didn't seem to be born with natural driving talent, but he was willing to pay his dues to learn the trade. He knocked around area short tracks, and by age 25 had a respectable BGN ride. Finally, he caught the attention of Cale Yarborough who offered him an opportunity to drive his WC Oldsmobiles and Pontiacs. This gig lasted for two seasons with mediocre results at best. Jarrett's big break came in 1990 when Neil Bonnett's injuries kept him from driving the Wood brothers' Citgo Fords. Jarrett had the nod as a replacement driver. The next two seasons weren't especially memorable as Jarrett scored only one victory and three top fives.

When legendary National Football League coach Joe Gibbs decided to enter NASCAR racing, crew chief–designate Jimmy Makar (Jarrett's brother-in-law) convinced "the coach" to put DJ behind the wheel. In the second year of operation, Dale confirmed the Makar/Gibbs decision by winning the 1993 Daytona 500. Who can forget father Ned calling the last lap on the live CBS broadcast?

Jarrett had a one-term contract with Gibbs Racing, but in 1994 when Irvan was nearly killed in a practice accident in Michigan, it was obvious that Yates would need a temporary replacement. Jarrett saw the No. 28 ride as his possible ticket to a championship. The remainder of the 1994 season and through 1995, Jarrett and the No. 28 team struggled. Team members weren't happy with him, and the press and public constantly belittled his efforts.

In late 1995, Robert Yates decided he would field a second team. When it looked like Jarrett was headed back down the motorsports food chain, Yates gave him a second chance. Teamed with rookie crew chief Todd Parrott and solid Ford sponsorship, Jarrett came out of the box with both barrels blazing. Winning the 1996 Daytona 500 in convincing style and chalking up seven season victories propelled the No. 88 team to third in points. Suddenly, WC had another superteam on their hands.

ROBERT YATES RACING

Whenever possible, save the packaging from your diecast cars. This special Batman/Joker series from Action Performance and Revell Collection are no exception.

Shown above is the colorful packaging for three No. 36 Pontiacs, in three scales, as driven by Ernie Irvan.

After his dominating run to the WC title in 1999, Jarrett and the No. 88 team only finished fourth in points for 2000. But third, second, third, first, and fourth (in WC points) in five years is the kind of consistency that marks a perennial championship contender. The No. 88 team, with the new colors of UPS for the 2001 season, would seem to again be a solid threat for their second WC title in the new season.

Kenny Irwin

Kenny Irwin was in the midst of his third year in NASCAR's premier division WC in 2000. He got his big break in 1998 when he was named the replacement for Ernie Irvan to drive the No. 28 Texaco/Havoline Ford. Irwin left the Yates operation at the end of the 1999 season to join Felix Sabates' Team Sabco and drive the Bell South No. 42 Chevy.

Irwin's life and career ended on July 7, 2000, at New Hampshire Speedway during practice prior to qualifying. The young Indiana native was killed instantly when his race car slammed into the third turn wall at over 150 miles per hour. It marked the second time in two months that tragedy occurred in nearly the same location. Fourth-generation driver Adam Petty died of multiple injuries in a very similar incident in preparation for a BGN race at the New England 1-mile track.

Irwin began driving go-karts as a youth and worked his way up through the ranks to high-powered open-wheel race cars. In five seasons in the United States Auto Club (USAC) National Midget Series, Irwin had 8 wins, 20 second-place finishes, 59 top fives, and 87 top tens to his credit. Irwin capped his open-wheel career with the 1996 USAC Skoal National Midget Series championship. In 1997, Irwin drove the No. 98 Raybestos Ford in the NASCAR Craftsman Truck Series (CTS). He was named Rookie-of-the-Year, won twice, and finished 10th in the season's points standings.

When petroleum giant Texaco was looking to replace Ernie Irvan, Irwin was strongly recommended. While driving the No. 28 Taurus for Yates, Irwin won Rookie-of-the-Year honors in 1998. Unfortunately, although many

NASCAR DIECAST AND MODEL CARS

Both Action Performance and Revell Collection rendered the 1998 Batman/Joker paint schemes into 1/24th-scale diecast replicas as used in the World 600 on the No. 28 and No. 88 Fords.

thought the magical success enjoyed by fellow open-wheel star Jeff Gordon might be repeated, it didn't happen for Irwin. His career never really got out of low gear. In two years with Yates, Irwin had 87 starts with no wins, three poles, and only four top-five finishes.

Ricky Rudd

Beginning with the 2000 NASCAR WC season, Virginia native Ricky Rudd assumed the driving chores for one of the most storied and respected stock cars currently on the circuit, the No. 28 Texaco/Havoline Ford Taurus. After six years as one of the few driver/owners in this highly competitive series, Rudd seemed like the perfect matchup for the starstruck Robert Yates No. 28 team. Rudd is probably best known these days for his 15 consecutive seasons with at least one victory, and his victory in the 1997 Brickyard 400 at Indianapolis Motor Speedway.

Rudd's entryway to stock car racing's major leagues came about through his father. Al Rudd operated an auto salvage business where young Ricky cultivated his affinity for things automotive. As a boy, Ricky cut his teeth on motocross bike competition, and in the late 1960s, behind the wheel of a go-kart.

Rudd's first competitive start in a NASCAR event came at Charlotte Motor Speedway (now called Lowe's Motor Speedway) in October 1980. Rudd qualified second in a family-owned race car, ran well all day, and finished fourth. That exposure directly led to the offer of a full-time ride in the No. 88 DiGard machine.

Rudd was selected as NASCAR Rookie-of-the-Year in 1977. He went on to drive for Richard Childress in the early 1980s. Rudd won for the first time on the road course at the now-defunct Riverside International Raceway in California. It was Rudd's first trip to victory lane in a NASCAR event, and it also marked the first victory for Childress as an owner.

Since that time, Rudd has piloted race cars for Bud Moore, Kenny Bernstein, and Rick Hendrick. Rudd drove the Motorcraft No. 15 Ford for Moore to many victories. When drag-racing ace Kenny Bernstein took a turn at team ownership in NASCAR WC, Rudd piloted the No. 26 Buick.

ROBERT YATES RACING

Shown here are a pair of Quaker State No. 26 Buicks as driven by Ricky Rudd for drag racer Kenny Bernstein in 1989. Wayne Moyer built this No. 26 Buick Regal on the left from a Starter kit. Mike Madlinger built this 1/24th-scale No. 26 on the right from a Monogram kit.

After he worked for auto magnate Rick Hendrick, Rudd won races including finishing a close second in the 1991 season points to champ Dale Earnhardt. In 1992, Rudd took the measure of the best foreign and domestic racers by winning that season's International Race of Champions (IROC) four-race series.

In 1994, Rudd left the Hendrick operation to become the owner/driver of the team owned by himself and his wife. Rudd struck a deal with Ford and was able to maintain his good standing with Procter & Gamble's Tide soap brand to continue as his sponsor. When multi-car teams eventually became the road to success, Rudd began to find the one-car team approach most difficult. The breaking point came when a new upstart team managed to negotiate the Tide sponsor away from Rudd Performance Motorsports. The deal with Robert Yates Racing was the bright light at he end of the tunnel.

At the close of the 2000 NASCAR WC season, Rudd had 19 career victories. He finished fifth behind teammate Dale Jarrett in the battle for the multimillion-dollar 2000 season championship. The record book also shows 2 poles, 12 top fives, and 19 top tens in Rudd's column.

Introduction to Collectibles

No. 28

When Davey Allison came to the No. 28 team after Yates became the owner, numerous plastic kits and diecast models were produced. The French company Starter manufactured a pair of 1/43rd-scale resin kits of Allison's 1987 and 1991 rides. Revell-Monogram recently expanded their list of No. 28 model kits by offering a replica of Allison's 1987 Havoline T-Bird that includes a prepainted resin figure of the late driver. Even in death, Allison remains extremely popular, as do the diecast models and plastic kits of his race cars. Fortunately, his tragic death has not set the price and availability of such items at a premium.

Ernie Irvan took over the No. 28 ride after Allison's death. A variety of plastic kits and diecast models were produced bearing Irvan's name. Revell-Monogram, Hot Wheels, and Revell Collection are just three of the manufacturers that have immortalized Irvan's time behind the wheel of the No. 28 Ford. Starter is responsible for a resin 1/43rd-scale kit of the 1995 Havoline T-Bird.

NASCAR DIECAST AND MODEL CARS

Hasbro's Winner's Circle series features two Dale Jarrett items. The Deluxe Series (left) celebrates the 2000 Daytona 500 victory. The other items show him winning the "Winston Million" in the Winston 500 at Talledega in 1998.

Kenny Irwin replaced Ernie Irvan in the No. 28 starting with the 1998 season. Although he won the rookie title, it was a lackluster season at best. The No. 28 Taurus was a very popular subject with manufacturers, and diecast products were produced in a wide variety of scales and price ranges from 1/64th to 1/18th.

Ricky Rudd is the current pilot of the No. 28 Havoline Ford. Starting with the 2000 season, 1/64th-scale and a choice of 1/24th-scale diecast models have been produced by Hasbro, Revell Collection, and Action Performance.

It had been a few seasons since a plastic kit had been produced of the No. 28 car, but a predecorated glue kit of the 2001 Texaco/Havoline race car was released by Revell in spring 2001.

No. 88

The No. 88 team started business in 1996 and hasn't changed the basic paint scheme to a great extent. A great number of T-Bird and Taurus models have closely followed along each year since the team began racing for Robert Yates.

One of the more rare plastic kits is the 1/24th scale Revell 1998 No. 88 Ford Taurus. Word has it that slightly less than 5,000 pieces were produced of this item.

For 2001, Revell unveiled a 1/24th scale Pro-Finish glue kit of the new UPS No. 88 paint scheme. Without question, diecast manufacturers will do a plethora of scales and price ranges for this new No. 88 paint treatment.

ROBERT YATES RACING

Above: Both Action Performance and Revell Collection produced diecast versions of the Batman/Joker paint schemes used on the No. 88 in the 1998 World 600 at Lowe's Motor Speedway. The Action Performance 1/24th scale is on the left, and Revell Collection's 1/43rd scale is on the right.

Left: Tom Dill built this 1/24th-scale replica of the 1996 T-Bird Dale Jarrett drove to victory in the Daytona 500. Dill used Revell-Monogram kit No. 2472.

Top left: Mark Martin stays in touch with the family in Florida.

Bottom left: Matt Kenseth won the 2000 Rookie-of-the-Year title.

Above right: Jeff Burton drives the No. 99 Citgo Taurus for Roush Racing.

8

Roush Racing

Jack Roush has certainly come a long way since graduating from Kentucky's Berea College in the early-1960s. Currently, he owns Roush Industries, which is home to 1,300 employees, and has one million square feet of facilities in four states. Through the 2000 season, Roush also operated five Winston Cup (WC) teams, two Busch Grand National (BGN) teams, and two Craftsman Truck Series (CTS) teams in NASCAR competition.

Roush, who holds a degree in mathematics, was hired in the engineering department at Ford Motor Company in 1964. While he was there, Roush quickly gravitated to an eclectic group of fellow engineers who called themselves the "Fastbacks." This group had interests in drag racing at the height of the musclecar era in the late 1960s.

At Ford, Roush developed a solid reputation for building powerful racing engines that won. By the early 1970s, Roush was busy constructing a successful drag racing team with fellow enthusiast Wayne Gapp. The Gapp and Roush team won the International Hot Rod Association (IHRA) Pro Stock World Championship in 1973 and 1974.

Since that time, Roush teams have captured over 20 championships in many levels of major-league motorsports. With the exception of the NASCAR WC title, Roush race teams have taken titles in Sports Car Club of America (SCCA) Trans-Am (T/A) events, International Motor Sports Association (IMSA) races, and multiple victories in international road-racing events including the 24 Hours of Daytona.

In the late 1990s, Roush Racing fielded Mustangs for four-time T/A champ Tommy Kendall. Kendall succeeded in winning the title a record three years in a row, and in 1997 he won 11 races in a row on his way to the SCCA T/A title.

Roush began fielding a single WC team for Mark Martin in Stroh Lite Thunderbirds in 1988. Martin continued to pilot Fords for Roush, which carried Stroh livery in 1988 and 1989, Folgers sponsorship from 1991 through 1993, and Valvoline livery through the 2000 season on the WC tour. Although it hasn't captured a title to date, the Roush/Martin team has finished in the top ten in points for 12 straight years, and finished second in 1990, 1994, and 1998.

Roush always has been a believer in "safety in numbers," fielding multi-car teams over the years with great success. Although he has entered multiple teams in WC, it wasn't until the 2000 season that this concept paid dividends for Roush. The Roush operation fielded CTS teams for Greg Biffle and Kurt Busch this past year. Biffle captured the 2000 CTS championship, while rookie Busch finished a close second.

For 2001, Roush Racing trimmed his WC operation back to only four teams. Biffle moved to the BGN series and drove a Granger Taurus. Busch took over the driving duties in the No. 97 Taurus to compete for the WC Rookie-of-the-Year title. Promising newcomers Nathan Haseleu and Chuck Hossfeld will move into the vacated Roush CTS racing trucks for the new season.

Mark Martin

Arguably, Mark Martin may be the most competitive driver ever to compete in NASCAR WC and not have won the championship title. Martin has driven Fords for Jack Roush since 1988. Although he hasn't captured a title to date, the Roush/Martin team has finished in the top ten in championship points for 12 straight years, and placed second in 1990, 1994, and 1998.

At the age of 15, Martin began his racing career driving a 1955 Chevy on the dirt tracks and short-paved bull rings around his Batesville, Arkansas, home. Today, most teens are not able to even possess a driver's license, let alone drive a race

75

NASCAR DIECAST AND MODEL CARS

The Revell Collection created this pair of 1/18th-scale diecast replicas of Mark Martin's No. 6. The 1997 Valvoline T-Bird is on the left, and the 1997 Winn-Dixie BGN ride of Mark Martin is on the right.

car! Before he was 18, Martin's career was well along as he hot-lapped to numerous feature wins and track championships.

In 1977, Martin began racing in the American Speed Association (ASA). The young speed merchant was named Rookie-of-the-Year. Martin capitalized on this momentum and went on to win the 1978 season championship.

With three ASA titles under his belt, Martin had accumulated enough confidence and financial backing to tackle his ultimate goal—NASCAR WC competition. In 1981, Martin entered five WC races. He raced to a third-place finish in the Martinsville, Virginia, event. Winner Darrell Waltrip and second-place Harry Gant were the only regulars to finish on the lead lap.

Martin sold all of his ASA equipment, made a total commitment to the series in 1982, and drove his own equipment with sponsorship from Cherokee wood-burning stoves.

He did record a few top tens and even two in the top five. He finished second to Geoff Bodine in the rookie title competition. The team's books showed he had won nearly $125,000 when they closed up shop.

For 1983, Martin was hired on to drive for a team backed by J. D. Stacy, and he was fired seven races into the season. This was followed by a six-race stint with a newly formed Morgan-McClure team. Just that quick, Martin found himself out of a job and headed back to Arkansas empty handed.

Martin regrouped by building some new aero-style Ford Thunderbirds and took advantage of a weight reduction rule the ASA had adopted to encourage participation from non-GM race cars. Martin signed a lucrative sponsorship deal with Miller Brewing and won his fourth ASA title in 1986.

ROUSH RACING

Wayne Doebling built this Mark Martin 1996 Valvoline Ford replica from the 1/24th-scale Monogram kit No. 2477.

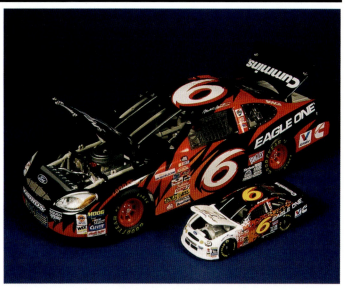

Here's a pair of Team Caliber diecast Mark Martin No. 6 Taurus race cars. On the left is the 1/24th-scale Eagle One paint scheme that was run at Talladega in 2000. On the right is the 1/64th-scale 1999 Eagle One paint scheme from the Brickyard 400.

In 1988, Roush began fielding a single WC team for Martin. Since then, Martin has raced Fords for Roush under Stroh livery in 1988 and 1989, Folgers from 1991 through 1993, Valvoline through the 2000 season and in 2001, and Pfizer-brand Viagra on the No. 6 Roush Taurus.

Martin's career statistics through the 2000 season show that he has 32 WC victories. He won the International Race of Champions (IROC) series title in 1994, 1996, 1997, and 1998. In the NASCAR BGN series, Martin is the all-time event winner with 45 victories. His four ASA championships came in 1978, 1979, 1980, and 1986.

After recent season-winning multiple races, Martin experienced an off-year in 2000 with only a single victory. The new sponsorship contract with Pfizer reportedly includes a $5 million bonus for Martin should he win the NASCAR WC championship.

Jeff Burton

By all accounts, Jeff Burton is championship material and ripe to win the NASCAR WC title any year now. Burton drives the No. 99 Citgo Ford Taurus for Roush Racing. Fellow competitors take him seriously as a week-to-week contender for the victory. To date in NASCAR's top league, Burton has recorded 15 WC victories, 82 top fives, 120 top tens, and over $5 million in winnings in his six years on the circuit.

After finishing fourth in 1997 (his first season with Roush), and fifth in 1998 and 1999, Burton completed the 2000 NASCAR season in third place for the championship with five victories and over $5 million in winnings. Late in the season, the familiar and colorful Exide paint scheme was replaced by the patriotic colors of Citgo on the No. 99 Ford.

Jeff Burton traces his keen racing interest to when he was five and would watch older brother Ward at the wheel of

NASCAR DIECAST AND MODEL CARS

Wayne Doebling built this pair of 1/24th-scale replicas of T-Birds driven by Jeff Burton. The car on the left is the Raybestos No. 8 owned by the Stavola Brothers race team. On the right is the 1997 Exide Ford owned by Roush Racing. Both vehicles were built from a Monogram Thunderbird kit and aftermarket decals.

This pair of Jeff Burton 1/24th-scale No. 99 Exide plastic kits. The Revell snap kit (No. 1314) is on the left, and the Revell glue kit (No. 2558) is on the right.

a go-kart. Eventually, Jeff began racing go-karts and won the state championship title twice before graduating into stock cars. Jeff ran in the NASCAR Winston Racing Series and recorded 21 wins before moving up to the BGN series in 1989. Jeff posted 4 wins, 15 top-fives, and 3 poles in his five seasons in BGN.

Jeff ran his first WC race at New Hampshire Speedway in 1993 and caught the attention of the Stavola brothers' operation. He began his WC career full-time for the team in 1994, and qualified for all but one event on his way to win the coveted rookie title, besting, among others, his older brother Ward.

When Roush entertained the idea of expanding to a three-car operation, Jeff Burton became his main focus for the driving chores. Burton jumped at the chance to join the Roush juggernaut. The No. 99 Exide Fords were housed in the same Mooresville complex as Mark Martin's No. 6 Valvoline machines.

Since he joined Roush, Burton has matured into a consistent front-runner with 15 wins, 82 top-fives, and 120 top-tens. Burton is also responsible for over $15 million in total winnings added to the coffers at Roush Racing. In 1999, the No. 99 Exide team with Burton at the wheel also captured a pair of the No Bull million-dollar bonuses.

The only soft spot in the No. 99 arsenal seems to be their frequent tendency in performing poorly during Bud pole qualifying. With the exception of the occasional mechanical failure, improvement during first-day qualifying would go a long way toward putting Burton into weekly contention for the NASCAR Winston Cup title.

The remarkable ability of the No. 99 team to recover and come from behind seems to be one of Burton's strongest attributes. In many of the events during the 1999 and 2000 season, Burton put on an amazing and inspired charge to the front. As his stats reflect, finishing near the front is not a problem for this team. Imagine how competitive the No. 99

ROUSH RACING

A trio of Jeff Burton Exide No. 99 Fords feature the 1997 1/43rd-scale T-Bird by Revell Collection (left), the Team Caliber 1/64th-scale 1998 Taurus (center), and the Racing Champions 1996 T-Bird in 1/144th scale (right).

Citgo team will be in the 2001 season if they can deal with their past shortcomings.

Matt Kenseth

Matt Kenseth finished out 2000, his first full season in NASCAR WC racing, 14th in points. Kenseth managed to best much-heralded fellow first-year contender Dale Earnhardt Jr. for the Raybestos Rookie-of-the-Year title. His one victory, along with 4 top-five and 11 top-ten finishes, propelled him to over $2 million in winnings.

During a ceremony at the Roush Racing shop, Wisconsin native Kenseth received a special leather jacket to commemorate his new "crown," and was later presented a $50,000 prize from the Raybestos Brakes Corporation.

Kenseth and the younger Earnhardt had been friendly rivals for a couple of years in the BGN series. There, Earnhardt Jr. beat Kenseth and won the series championship back to back in 1998 and 1999.

Ironically, the tables were turned for the youthful competitors during the 2000 WC season. Kenseth captured the rookie title with consistency, which is the foundation of NASCAR competition. From the beginning of the 2000 season, Kenseth slowly rose to the top of the rookie contenders' chart. He had four top tens in the last half of the season and two less DNFs than Earnhardt Jr.

Kenseth was brought to the attention of team owner Jack Roush through longtime NASCAR driver Mark Martin. Martin, greatly impressed with the 28 year old's on-track talents and general race car savvy, has mentored Kenseth for the last few years. Martin persuaded Roush to sign Kenseth, and is co-owner of the No. 17 DeWalt Fords Kenseth drives.

Kenseth competed in the BGN series driving for Robby Reiser in the DeWalt Chevy. He carried the sponsorship with him to the senior series. During the 1999 season, Kenseth ran five events in the No. 17 1999 Taurus before he competed full-time in the 2000 DeWalt Taurus.

NASCAR DIECAST AND MODEL CARS

Many diecast manufacturers have jumped on the Matt Kenseth bandwagon. Shown here are two 1/64th-scale diecast models of the 1999 Hot Wheels (left) and 2000 Racing Champions (right) Tauruses.

Team Caliber produced these three 1/24th-scale diecast models of DeWalt-sponsored Fords. At left is the 1999 Taurus, only available by mail order from Roush Racing. The standard 2000 paint scheme is on the center vehicle. At right is the 1999 Robby Riser–owned Monte Carlo driven by Kenseth in the BGN series.

Greg Biffle

Greg Biffle captured the 2000 NASCAR CTS title in convincing style. This feat marked the very first NASCAR championship for Jack Roush and Roush Racing. Twice before the Roush operation was poised to celebrate their first trip to the "head table" when misfortune struck. Controversial penalties involving intake manifolds foiled Mark Martin's title hopes in 1990. In spite of a record nine wins for Biffle in 1999, a similar infraction denied him the CTS title.

Biffle has competed in the NASCAR CTS for three years since he joined Roush. So far he has entered 76 events with 14 wins. Biffle has added to that 40 top-fives and 49 top-ten finishes on his way to $1.5 million in winnings.

Roush has never doubted the wisdom of hiring the former short-track champion from Portland, Oregon. In 1996, Biffle won 27 of the 47 events he entered in the West Coast NASCAR short-track series.

Biffle's sterling efforts during the 1996 Winter Heat series in Tucson, Arizona, caught the eye of former NASCAR WC champ-turned-broadcaster Benny Parsons. Parsons was so impressed with Biffle's on-track skills that he felt compelled to address the subject with Roush. What Roush heard was that Parsons considered Biffle to be the best natural talent he had seen in 40 years.

For 2001, Biffle moved from the CTS to the Busch series and took sponsor Granger with him. Biffle will pilot the Roush No. 60 Taurus vacated at the end of the 2000 season by Mark Martin.

Introduction to Collectibles
No. 6

The 1990 Folgers T-Bird kit was one of the first No. 6 Ford plastic kit releases and was produced by Revell-Monogram. This was followed by a string of Valvoline Fords reproduced in 1/24th-scale plastic by AMT and Revell-Monogram. Virtually every year and paint scheme for the No. 6 Valvoline car have been offered in model kit form. The few paint layouts in over-the-counter kits have come

ROUSH RACING

These are two No. 16 Roush Fords. Rear: a Team Caliber 1/24th-scale FamilyClick.com driven by Kevin Lapage in 2000. Front: a Hot Wheels 1/64th-scale Primestar Taurus driven by Ted Musgrave.

from aftermarket decal manufacturers such as Fred Cady Design and SLIXX.

The Ertl company's 1/18th-scale diecast Valvoline T-Bird was one of the very first releases in what would become a multimillion-dollar diecast collectibles market. Hot Wheels, Racing Champions, Revell Collection, and Team Caliber have all produced a broad range of No. 6 Mark Martin Fords. Some of these companies have released limited quantities of some of the best-looking special paint schemes.

In spite of the sponsor changing to Pfizer's Viagra brand, look for many of these manufacturers to offer high-quality diecast and plastic glue-type model kits.

No. 99

Although the No. 99 Ford has only been on the circuit since 1997, there is a good selection to choose from. Revell-Monogram and AMT have both offered plastic kits of race cars driven by Jeff Burton. Revell-Monogram has also offered pre-decorated snap kits of this racer. Aftermarket decal makers have produced water-slide decals to re-create many of Jeff Burton's rides, even decals that came before his tenure at Roush.

Diecast models of the No. 99 Exide Fords have been produced in many scales and by a variety of manufacturers since 1997. Team Caliber, Ertl, Revell Collection, and Racing Champions have offered 1/64th-, 1/43rd-, 1/24th-, and 1/18th-scale Exide racing vehicles. Team Caliber was one of the first to produce a replica of the midseason sponsor change to the 2000 No. 99 Citgo markings.

No. 97, 26, 17, 16, Etc.

Farm equipment manufacturer John Deere signed on to sponsor Chad Little a year before he joined the Roush stables. The Ertl company produced a 1/18th-scale diecast of the 1997 John Deere Pontiac. Many diecast manufacturers joined in after Little's operation was bought out by Jack Roush. John Deere Pontiacs and Fords have been the subject of medium- and large-scale diecast replicas in many price ranges. John Deere terminated its relationship with Roush after the 2000

NASCAR DIECAST AND MODEL CARS

These diecast No. 30 Pennzoil Pontiacs are replicas of the car Johnny Benson drove for Bahari Racing for the 1996 and 1997 seasons. Shown here are a Ertl 1/18th-scale 1997, a Revell Collection 1/24th-scale 1996, a Revell Collection 1/43rd-scale 1997, and a Racing Champions 1997 in 1/144th scale.

This is to date the lone 1/24th-scale No. 97 John Deere plastic glue kit. This 1997 Pontiac Grand Prix is Revell-Monogram kit No. 2492.

Revell had two 1/24th-scale kit versions of the 1998 No. 26 Cheerios Taurus driven by Johnny Benson. The snap kit on the left is No. 85-1316, and the glue kit version on the right is No. 2553.

ROUSH RACING

A pair of 1997 No. 97 John Deere Pontiacs consists of a Revell Collection 1/43rd-scale signature series and a 1/24th-scale Revell Select series that was run at the 1997 Brickyard 400 to commemorate John Deere's 160th anniversary (front).

season. Kurt Busch will drive the No. 97 in 2001. At this writing, no sponsor has been identified for this car.

Matt Kenseth has only been on the scene for a brief period. Team Caliber, Hot Wheels, and Racing Champions have produced diecast cars of the DeWalt Fords. Team Caliber has made both the BGN Chevy and the WC 1999 and 2000 Taurus. Hot Wheels did the 1999 car in 1/64th scale. Racing Champions in turn offered the 2000 car in 1/64th scale.

John Benson was with the Roush operation for 1998 and 1999. The Cheerios team No. 26 had little success during that period and ceased operations after the 1999 season. However, at least two plastic glue kits and some diecast replicas of this short-lived team exist.

Other drivers, including Wally Dallenbach Jr., Ted Musgrave, and Kevin Lapage, have piloted the No. 16 Fords for Roush under a variety of primary sponsors. Revell-Monogram produced a 1/24th-scale plastic kit of the Family Channel T-Bird. Hot Wheels and Team Caliber have issued diecast models in 1/64th and 1/24th-scale of the No. 16 car as driven by Lapage and Musgrave. This Roush team will not exist for the 2001 season.

Roush Trucks

Roush Racing trucks have been driven by the likes of Joe Ruttman, Chuck Bown, Greg Biffle, and Kurt Busch. To date, there have been just a few pieces representing these Craftsman series vehicles.

Jeremy Mayfield drives the No. 12 Mobile 1 Ford Taurus for Penske.

The 1989 NASCAR WC champion, Rusty Wallace.

9

Penske Racing

Roger Penske

One of today's most successful businessmen, Roger Penske began his racing career at Akron Speedway, and he quickly followed that with a successful run in Sports Car Club of America (SCCA) road racing. Penske always has believed in setting his goals far beyond what he could reasonably expect to accomplish. He soon realized that he could possess anything he wanted if he could generate enough capital. In the early years, Penske made money by buying, racing, and selling dozens of cars.

When he decided to exit the driver's seat, Penske teamed up with graduate engineer and promising racer Mark Donohue. Together the duo pushed the envelope in virtually every type of racing they competed in. They won the Indy 500 for the first time in 1972. Together they won two SCCA Trans-Am titles. Their impressive wins in road racing include the 24 Hours of Daytona in 1969 and NASCAR at Riverside in 1973. To date, Penske Racing has won 10 Indy 500s and recorded over 100 victories in open-wheel competition alone.

Penske's first venture into NASCAR saw some measured success with American Motors Matadors. Drivers like Donohue, Gary Bettenhausen, Dave Marcis, and Bobby Allison helped the team capture five wins between 1972 and 1976. In 1980, Penske fielded Chevrolets twice for a young and promising St. Louis native—Rusty Wallace. At Atlanta that year Wallace finished a close second to eventual winner Dale Earnhardt.

When Penske was coaxed back into NASCAR, he teamed up with longtime business associate Don Miller and Rusty Wallace to field a No. 2 Miller Pontiac Grand Prix. Over 30 of Wallace's current 53 victories in WC racing have happened since he joined Penske Racing in 1991.

In 1994, Penske Racing jumped the General Motors and Pontiac ship and switched to Ford Thunderbirds to carry the No. 2 Miller Lite livery. Although the Penske South team has continually been competitive by winning races and pole positions, they have not shown the kind of consistency that saw double-digit victories in the early 1990s.

Roger Penske purchased Nazareth Speedway, Michigan International Speedway, and North Carolina Motor Speedway before he built California Speedway in 1997. The new facility sits on an old Kaiser steel processing facility.

Penske was one of the first people in racing to make a public offering of stock in his motorsports operations. In 1999, Penske agreed to merge his racing facility holdings by folding them into those of the International Speedway Corporation that owns tracks including Daytona, Darlington, and Talladega. In 2000, Penske acquired the remaining interests of the Michael Kranefuss No. 12 Mobile 1 team in which Penske South had been part owner. In preparation for the 2001 season, Penske South continues forward as a two-car operation with Rusty Wallace in the Miller Lite No. 2 Ford and Jeremy Mayfield driving the No. 12 Mobile 1 Taurus.

Rusty Wallace

Rusty Wallace is one of the most motivated competitors in motorsports today. He currently ranks very close to the top ten in career victories in NASCAR WC with 53 wins. His first year in the series (1984), he captured the Rookie-of-the-Year title. He's only finished out of the top ten in the season's championship points totals once since his first win in 1986 at Bristol, Tennessee.

Wallace started out on the bull rings around the St. Louis area and eventually graduated to a more highly competitive series in the late 1970s. Wallace was the United States Auto Club (USAC) stock car Rookie-of-the-Year in 1979.

NASCAR DIECAST AND MODEL CARS

Rusty Wallace's first WC victory came at Bristol, Tennessee, in April 1986. This is a pair of 1986 Alugard Pontiac 2+2s. I built the 1/24th-scale version (rear) using an aftermarket resin body shell over a Monogram GM chassis with Fred Cady Design decals. Wayne Moyer built the 1/43rd-scale version from a Starter resin kit.

He also finished in second place in the championship chase that year. Between 1979 and 1982, Wallace frequented the nation's short tracks and traveled from Florida to California with considerable success. He racked up nearly 200 feature victories during this period in his blossoming career.

In 1980, Wallace caught the eye of Roger Penske who twice fielded Chevrolets for the young and promising St. Louis native. In 1983, Wallace joined the American Speed Association (ASA) circuit where he won eight races, four poles, and finished nearly 97 percent of the laps that season. His consistency propelled him to the series championship

title that year. His success in ASA opened up an opportunity with the Cliff Stewart team in the NASCAR WC series in 1984. Wallace was very consistent and was the class of the rookie field and claimed the 1984 Rookie-of-the-Year title. Wallace recorded his first of many career victories in 1986 driving the Raymond Beadle–owned Kodiak Pontiac 2+2 in the spring event at Bristol Motor Speedway.

Roger Penske was coaxed back into NASCAR in 1991 and teamed up with longtime business associate Don Miller and Rusty Wallace. The new Penske South operation began fielding black No. 2 Miller Pontiacs in the WC series. Over

NASCAR DIECAST AND MODEL CARS

Shown here are two pairs of

30 of Wallace's current 53 victories in WC racing have happened since joining forces with Penske in 1991.

In 1994, Penske Racing left the Pontiac camp, switched to Ford Thunderbirds, and continued to carry the No. 2 Miller Lite livery. Although Wallace and the Penske South team have remained competitive and have won races and pole positions, they have not shown the kind of consistency that saw 18 victories in 1993 and 1994 when they ran the Pontiac Grand Prix.

In the 2000 season, Wallace showed flashes of competitiveness that elevated him to superstardom in major league stock car racing. He won four times in 2000, captured a record nine pole positions, and led the most laps. Wallace finished seventh in NASCAR WC points in 2000.

Jeremy Mayfield

At age 13, Jeremy Mayfield had a taste of competition racing in go-karts. Later, running in the NASCAR WC Racing series, young Mayfield was known as a resourceful and friendly sort who protected his equipment and generally managed to survive to the checkered flag. He became a popular fixture in his part of the country at places like Nashville

NASCAR DIECAST AND MODEL CARS

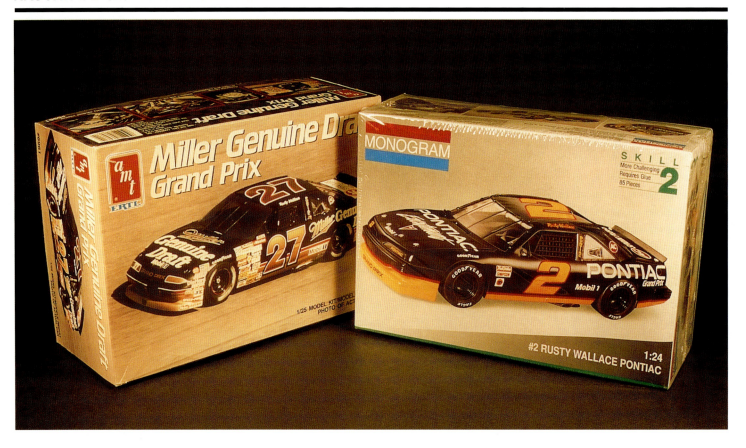

So far there are just two Rusty Wallace plastic stock car model kits available: AMT's 1/25th-scale kit No. 6961 (left) and Monogram's 1/24th-scale kit No. 2960 (right). The "politically correct" body graphics make no mention of Miller's sponsorship on the Monogram kit box art.

Fairgrounds Speedway and Whiteville, Tennessee. Then he moved on to the Midwest-based Automobile Racing Club of America (ARCA) stock car series recording 8 top fives and 10 top tens. His season performance garnered him the 1993 ARCA Rookie-of-the-Year title.

Former NASCAR WC champion Cale Yarborough quickly took note of Mayfield's exploits and hired him to drive his No. 98 Thunderbird. Mayfield recorded his first pole in 1996 at Talladega. In 1997, he joined the Kranefuss-Haas No. 37 team where he moved the team up to 18th in points by midseason.

Penske South bought out Carl Haas' interests in the Kranefuss-Haas operation in 1998. That same year Mobil 1 emerged as the primary sponsor on the race car which had its number changed from 37 to 12. That season Mayfield recorded 12 top fives and 16 top tens to go with an impressive first ever WC victory in the Pocono 500 on his way to seventh in points.

NASCAR DIECAST AND MODEL CARS

The Revell Collection Miller Lite diecast Fords of Rusty Wallace include a variety of paint schemes. The 2000 1/24th-scale standard paint scheme is pictured at the left, the 1997 1/43rd-scale Thunderbird with standard paint scheme is in the center, and the 1998 Elvis paint scheme in 1/64th scale, which first appeared at the Las Vegas Motor Speedway, is located at the right.

For 1999, the Mobil 1 team fell back a notch or two with no victories, 5 top fives, and only 12 top tens. The Mobil 1 team nearly matched their record season's earnings of 1998 by again taking in over $2 million in winnings. The 2000 season was a good news/bad news kind of deal for the Mobil 1 operation. Mayfield recorded two wins, but the team ran into problems with the NASCAR rule book. There was an unapproved fuel additive conflict at one race, and the car didn't pass post-race ride height inspection at the other.

Introduction to Collectibles
Rusty Wallace

Rusty Wallace came to NASCAR in the mid-1980s. Since then, there have been a limited number of kits of his race cars captured in miniature form. Among these few are the 1/43rd-scale resin kits from Starter which include the 1986 Alugard Pontiac and the 1989 Kodiak Grand Prix. It wasn't until 1992 that Starter revisited the subject. This French company then ran off a string of Wallace race cars in

NASCAR DIECAST AND MODEL CARS

These cars are replicas of the Kmart/RC Cola Fords Jeremy Mayfield drove before he joined the Penske team. Left to right: GMP (Ertl) 1997 Thunderbird (first full season with Kranefuss-Haas); 1/24th-scale 1997 Revell Collection; 1/43rd-scale Hasbro Winner's Circle; and 1/144th-scale Racing Champions version.

1/43rd scale like the 1992 Miller Pontiac Grand Prix and three Miller-sponsored Ford Thunderbirds.

For the builder of injection-molded plastic kits, the pickings are a bit more sparse. Model Products Corporation (MPC) offered the Alugard Pontiac in 1/25th scale as part of their Southern Stockers series in 1984. It wasn't until 1990 that AMT offered the No. 27 Miller Pontiac as part of their 1/25th-scale plastic kit line.

Since the mid-1990s, companies such as Action Performance and Revell Collection have filled the void with diecast replicas of many of Wallace's Pontiacs and Fords in a variety of scales and in many different price ranges. The Wallace mass-market diecast products do not display his sponsor's (Miller Brewing Company) product names or logo for fear of improper influence on young collectors.

Jeremy Mayfield

To date, there has not been a single plastic model kit of a Jeremy Mayfield NASCAR WC stock car in any scale. A couple of aftermarket decal sheets for cars driven before joining the No. 12 team have allowed modelers to replicate some of Mayfield's rides. There are a few No. 12 Mobil 1 diecast pieces from companies including Team Caliber, Action Performance, and Hasbro in their Winner's Circle line as driven by Jeremy Mayfield.

NASCAR DIECAST AND MODEL CARS

These vehicles are diecast No. 12 Jeremy Mayfield Mobil 1 Fords. A 1/24th-scale 1999 Team Caliber Taurus (left) and a Revell Collection 1/43rd-scale 1999 Taurus (right) are displayed in this photograph.

Consider displaying the colorful packaging and the diecast model together as part of your Jeremy Mayfield collection.

Tony Stewart grabbed the 1999 NASCAR Rookie-of-the-Year title by winning three races and finishing fifth in points.

Bobby Labonte won the coveted NASCAR WC championship in 2000.

10

Joe Gibbs Racing

Joe Gibbs

Joe Gibbs will long hold the distinction as the only person to have coached his team to three National Football League (NFL) Super Bowl victories, and then have his race team win the Daytona 500 and NASCAR WC championship. Gibbs' accomplishments in both the NFL and stock car racing have brought a near-priceless level of exposure to NASCAR racing.

Gibbs began to toy with the idea of fielding a NASCAR Winston Cup team back when he was winding down his professional football coaching career. Early on, Gibbs had managed to interest Interstate Batteries in being the primary sponsor of his race cars. Next, he met with Rick Hendrick and persuaded Hendrick to supply racing engines for the team that, thus far, only existed on paper.

Starting in 1992, Joe Gibbs Racing (JGR) began operations with Jimmy Makar as its first hire. Makar had a stellar reputation in the sport having been the chassis wizard on Rusty Wallace's championship team in 1989. Makar made finding a top driving prospect his number one goal. He didn't have to look too far as he is married to Dale Jarrett's sister.

By 1993, the Joe Gibbs team began to gel. The JGR operation showed that it was a threat early in the year by winning the Daytona 500 in only their second year of operation. The unforgettable final duel between Jarrett and Dale Earnhardt was broadcast live on CBS TV, and Dale's father, Ned, called the last lap shootout. That high-visibility victory helped propel the team to a fourth-place finish in the season's championship points chase.

The following year the proverbial "wheels" came off. Jarrett won only one race and finished a disappointing 16th in the points standings. Things worked out for the best after all as Jarrett left to take the open seat at Robert Yates Racing after Ernie Irvan's accident. This set in motion the move by Bobby Labonte from the Bill Davis team to the No. 18 Interstate Batteries Chevrolet.

For 1995, Labonte proved to be a contender, wrapping up the 10th spot in points by season's end, and recorded three wins. In 1996, the team only won once and finished 11th. Starting in 1997, the JGR team began a steady and consistent climb back toward the top as Bobby finished seventh in a new Pontiac, one spot behind his older brother Terry. Bobby moved up to the sixth spot in points in 1998 and won five races in 1999 on his way to challenge Dale Jarrett for the WC title.

"The coach," Joe Gibbs, was rewarded for his nine years of methodical struggles as Bobby recorded 4 victories, 19 top fives, and 24 top tens on his way to win the 2000 NASCAR WC championship.

Gibbs added a second team to the operation in 1999. Tony Stewart, another youthful open-wheel whiz kid from the Midwest, hit his stride early. By winning a record three races and finishing in the top five in points, Stewart easily won the 1999 Rookie-of-the-Year award. In 2000 the No. 20 Home Depot Pontiac was a frequent visitor to victory lane as Tony Stewart won a series-leading six races.

Bobby Labonte

Texan Bobby Labonte apparently was born with his fair share of racing genes. Just like his big brother Terry (seven years his senior), Bobby began racing in quarter-midgets at age five, which had become a family tradition. From the quarter-midgets, Bobby moved on to go-karts at age 14.

In 1979, the Labonte family moved from Texas to North Carolina when Bobby and Terry's father, Bob, was hired to work for the Billy Hagan NASCAR team that Terry

NASCAR DIECAST AND MODEL CARS

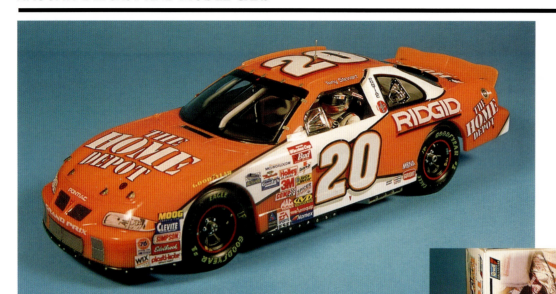

The author built this 1999 Home Depot Pontiac from the Revell kit No. 85-1646. He added a number of aftermarket parts including photo-etched hood pins, a roof-mounted two-way radio antenna, and the dry-break fuel filler on the left rear fender.

Tony Stewart collectibles are found in many scales and price ranges. Shown here are four examples in four different scales from Action Performance, Revell Collection, and Hasbro's Winner's Circle. Save these boxes because they add to the value of your diecast collectibles

drove for. After graduating from high school in 1982, Bobby went to work as a mechanic for Hagan's operation. In 1986, Terry left Hagan to work for Junior Johnson, and the other Labontes found themselves out on the street.

Bobby had made some contacts that led to working on and driving late-model stock cars. As part of a family-owned operation, Bobby moved to the Busch Grand National (BGN) series in 1990, and he won the championship the next season. While competing on the Busch circuit, Bobby became friends with Bill Davis, who was planning to move up to WC with his current driver, Jeff Gordon. When Rick Hendrick spirited Gordon away from Davis, the Maxwell House–sponsored ride was offered to Bobby.

When sponsorship looked like a problem for Davis, Bobby jumped at the opportunity to drive for Joe Gibbs Racing. The former NFL coach had recently lost his primary driver, Dale Jarrett, to the Robert Yates team. Bobby won three races in the Interstate Batteries Chevy that first season and finished 10th in points.

In 1996, Bobby finished the season with a victory at Atlanta. This same event that earned Terry his second WC title. For 1997, Joe Gibbs switched from Chevrolet to Pontiac.

NASCAR DIECAST AND MODEL CARS

Here are four examples in four different scales of Home Depot Pontiacs driven by Tony Stewart. Left to right: Action Performance 1/18th-scale Habitat for Humanity (as run in the UAW-GM 500 at Lowe's Motor Speedway in Charlotte, North Carolina); Revell Collection 1/24th-scale Rookie-of-the-Year paint scheme; Hasbro's Winner's Circle 1/43rd scale, Hasbro's New Stars of NASCAR 1/64th-scale series.

By 1999, Bobby was being touted as a serious threat to win the WC championship. He came close that season and gave eventual champion Dale Jarrett a contest throughout the season. By finally winning the championship for 2000, Bobby is the only NASCAR driver to win both the BGN title and the WC championship. The Interstate Batteries No. 18 is the first Pontiac race car to win the WC championship in 11 years.

In 2000, Bobby recorded 4 victories, 19 top fives, and 24 top tens to win his first WC title. For 2001, Bobby is firmly entrenched as the primary driver for Joe Gibbs, and it looks like a good bet that he will repeat his feats of the 2000 season.

Tony Stewart

This Rushville, Indiana, native began his career by racing go-karts. Like Tony Stewart, he didn't just race go-karts, he consumed the competition by capturing both the International Karting Foundation and World Karting Association national championship titles. Stewart then went on to three-quarter-midgets, followed by United States Auto Club (USAC) midget and sprint car competition.

Stewart, an accomplished race driver, developed as a regular competitor on televised motorsports. This type of exposure allowed him to pick from the most competitive rides available. Stewart won his first USAC National Midget Championship in 1994. In 1995, he became the first driver

NASCAR DIECAST AND MODEL CARS

The Revell Collection Rookie-of-the-Year diecast and Revell's prepainted glue-style plastic kit are two 1/24th-scale 1999 Tony Stewart Home Depot Pontiacs.

in series history to win all three of the top divisions—midget, sprint, and Silver Crown—all in the same year.

Stewart's accomplishments caught the eye of Team Menard while he competed in the newly formed Indy Racing League (IRL). He sat on the pole for his first Indy 500 in 1996. It's not surprising that the race organizers chose him as Rookie-of-the-Year. With a consistent performance, Stewart became the IRL's first homegrown champion in 1997.

While still competing in the IRL, Stewart was put under a NASCAR contract by Joe Gibbs Racing. Gibbs had acquired the BGN team formerly owned by Bobby Labonte. This situation was a perfect opportunity for Stewart to get experience in full-bodied race cars as Gibbs entered him in selected BGN events in 1998. Stewart, in his rookie season of NASCAR WC racing, won a record three races, finished fourth in points, and easily captured the Rookie-of-the-Year title.

In 2000, Stewart led all WC competitors with six victories. He added to that 12 top fives and 23 top tens to finish out the season in sixth place in points. For 2001, Stewart is positioned to challenge the likes of Burton, Jarrett, and his own teammate, Bobby Labonte, for the championship title.

Introduction to Collectibles

Joe Gibbs founded his Interstate team in 1992 with driver Dale Jarrett behind the wheel of No. 18. The first collectible items for the No. 18 car were an AMT 1/32nd-scale

NASCAR DIECAST AND MODEL CARS

Bobby Labonte and Dale Jarrett have both been behind the wheel of No. 18 Interstate Batteries Chevrolets. An Ertl 1/18th-scale 1995 Monte Carlo is on the left, and a 1992 Action Performance Lumina is on the right.

This is a special edition of the Ertl 1/18th-scale No. 18 Interstate Batteries Chevrolet Monte Carlo that was packaged for Easy Care Service Contracts.

NASCAR DIECAST AND MODEL CARS

Most Revell Collection diecast models are packaged and sold through hobby and collectibles stores and mail-order catalogs.

snap kit and 1/25th-scale glue kit. One of the first pieces of collectible diecast of the No. 18 Interstate Chevrolet Lumina came from Action Performance as part of their Racing Collectibles Club of America (RCCA) club offerings. Ertl followed with a 1/18th-scale 1995 Interstate Bobby Labonte Chevy from their American Muscle line.

After the team switched to Pontiacs in 1997, a string of diecast models followed from companies including Action Performance, Revell Collection, and Hasbro. Plastic kit builders had to settle for building the No. 18 race car using SLIXX aftermarket decals along with one of the new Revell-Monogram Pontiac Grand Prix 1/24th-scale kits.

In the late 1990s the Gibbs operation added a second team with rookie Tony Stewart. A few choice pieces of diecast emerged from manufacturers such as Revell Collection that included some of Stewart's BGN race cars. By 2000, additional diecast from a variety of producers was joined by four new plastic model kits of the Gibbs cars. In both their full-glue kit line and predecorated glue kit line, Revell released two pairs of excellent kits for the dedicated builder as well as the modeler of moderate skills.

Two very collectible items were released by British slot car specialists Scalextric. Both the No. 20 Home Depot and No. 18 Interstate Pontiacs are available in 1/32nd scale and look good screaming around a slot track as well as on a display case shelf.

NASCAR DIECAST AND MODEL CARS

Here's a quartet of No. 18 Bobby Labonte Pontiacs. The Revell Collection 1/18th scale marks the first race at Texas World Speedway and is part of the 1997 Revell Collection. Also displayed in this photograph are the Hot Rod *magazine paint scheme for the 1998 Daytona 500; Revell Collection's* Small Soldiers *movie paint scheme, as seen at Lowe's Motor Speedway in October 1999; and the 1/64th-scale Hasbro Winner's Circle standard 2000 paint scheme.*

Ward Burton, driver of the No. 22 CAT Dodge Intrepid.

Dave Blaney, driver of the No. 93 Amoco Dodge Intrepid.

11
Bill Davis Racing

Bill Davis

Arkansas native Bill Davis has been involved in racing since high school. Between 1969 and 1972, Davis raced motorcycles across the United States.

Davis grew up knowing Mark Martin and his father, Julian. Davis' dad and Julian were good friends. Julian Martin peaked Davis' interest in racing and the trucking business. Davis bought his first truck and went to work for Julian Martin by leasing his truck to Martin's company. While Davis worked as a dispatcher for JMI Trucking, he had the opportunity to help the Martins with their American Speed Association (ASA) program.

By 1987 Davis had started his own company, but he still had the racing bug. He had his first up-front taste of big-time stock car racing as a gas man on Mark Martin's NASCAR Apache Buick in 1982. That was a pivotal year for Davis, and he built a short-track team for Mark Martin to compete on in the ASA and ARTGO circuits.

Prior to the 1988 season, businessman/racer Jack Roush launched his own Winston Cup (WC) team and wanted Martin, who was fresh from winning the ASA championship for the third time, to drive his No. 6 Stroh-sponsored Ford Thunderbird. Davis wanted to somehow continue his involvement in stock car racing with Martin. He thought he could race in the Busch series if only he could find a sponsor. Mark Martin secured Carolina Ford Dealers who proposed a 15-race deal to back Davis.

The Davis Busch team had a great driver who was very knowledgeable about building and setting up a racecar. Martin and the Roush crew looked forward to expanding their experience by competing in the Busch car on Saturdays. Davis fielded Fords for Mark Martin and Jeff Gordon.

Davis has been the owner of a NASCAR WC team since 1993 when he secured the Maxwell House sponsorship for his No. 22 Pontiacs for driver Bobby Labonte. The long-awaited trip to victory lane in the NASCAR WC series for Bill Davis came in October 1995. Ward Burton, at the wheel of the Caterpillar No. 22 Pontiac Grand Prix, sped to the checkered flag at the North Carolina Motor Speedway in Rockingham, North Carolina. This win came just seven races into the relationship.

Bill Davis Racing (BDR) would appear to have all the ingredients for ultimate success, including an aggressive in-house engine-building program, multi-car team format, and a 130,000-square-foot state-of-the-art motorsports facility. This team combined a selection of prominent sponsors, cutting-edge technology, and gifted personnel to become a formidable force in NASCAR WC racing.

In 1999, Caterpillar began its tenure as the primary sponsor of the No. 22 BDR Pontiac Grand Prix, and Polaris joined on as major associate sponsor in 2000. Siemens moved over from the No. 22 team to become the major associate sponsor on the No. 93 car. Amoco continued as the major sponsor on No. 93. The AT&T sponsorship on the BDR full-time Busch series team gives this operation four sponsoring companies that rank in the top 160 on Fortune magazine's Global 500.

Entering the 2001 season, Davis is poised to make another quantum leap from General Motors' Pontiac division to become part of DaimlerChrysler's Dodge division's return to the NASCAR senior circuit. The CAT No. 22 and the No. 93 Amoco racecar will be part of the new Dodge contingent when the season opens at Daytona in February 2001. The BP-Amoco Ultimate brand continues its involvement with BDR as the primary sponsor on Dave Blaney's No. 93 Dodge Intrepid for 2001.

NASCAR DIECAST AND MODEL CARS

Right: These are 1/24th-scale diecast models of cars driven by Ward Burton early in his NASCAR career. A Racing Champions bank of the 1992 No. 2 Hardee's Chevy Lumina owned by A. G. Dillard that Burton drove in the BGN series is at the rear. A Racing Champions 1995 No. 31 Hardee's Chevy Lumina owned by A. G. Dillard is at the left. A 1996 Racing Champions No. 22 Maxwell House Pontiac owned by Bill Davis and driven by Burton is at the right.

Left: Saving the original packaging, such as these for Ward Burton diecast models, really adds to the value of your collectibles.

Ward Burton

After Bobby Labonte's departure for the Joe Gibbs team, Davis hired NASCAR Busch North standout Randy LaJoie. With a lackluster record by midseason, Davis replaced LaJoie with Ward Burton, who rejuvenated the team when he took the wheel late in the 1995 season. Teaming Ward Burton with Tommy Baldwin had the potential of great success when combined with financial support from primary sponsor Caterpillar.

Like his younger brother Jeff, Ward cut his racing teeth on the short track around his Virginia home. Ward started his Busch career with the A. G. Dilliard team in the No. 2 Chevy, and moved with that operation into Winston Cup with the No. 31 Hardees Chevy. Ward left the Dilliard operation in midseason to take the Davis seat when the team lost the Hardees sponsorship.

Eighth-year driver Ward and crew chief Tommy Baldwin Jr., one of the sport's most sought-after young talents, made up a formidable competitive nucleus that has propelled BDR to the upper echelons of motorsports. Ward has become one of the series most popular personalities, having won in this eighth start for BDR, and he is one of the significant foundational building blocks of structure and growth since 1995.

Ward struggles most often with his younger brother Jeff. Three times in 1999, the two Burton brothers battled down to the checkered flag. On all three occasions, Ward had to settle for second place.

The 2000 season held a lot of promise for the Davis team. Although Ward had no victories in 34 starts, the team had 6 top fives and a team record of 16 top tens on their way to ninth place in the points standings.

NASCAR DIECAST AND MODEL CARS

These CAT No. 22 kits feature different scales. The 1999 Revell 1/24th scale at the left is a full-glue-type plastic kit (No. 85-2992). The Racing Champions 1/64th-scale diecast kit, which is actually nothing more than an unassembled version of their factory-built piece, is shown at the right.

This quartet of 1/24th-scale diecast CAT 1999 Pontiacs is made by four different manufacturers: Action Performance, Hot Wheels, Hasbro, and Racing Champions.

Dave Blaney

Bill Davis again displayed his sharp eye for young talent by providing a first-rate opportunity for future stock car racing fixture Dave Blaney. Davis has an excellent track record in this regard having provided early-career NASCAR opportunities for current WC contenders Jeff Gordon, Mark Martin, Bobby Labonte, and Ward Burton

In the NASCAR Busch series, the 1995 World of Outlaws (WoO) champion Dave Blaney continued his successful transition from open-wheel cars to stock cars and has finished well in the top ten in the Busch points standings in only his third NASCAR season. The 2000 season marked the point at which Blaney became Ward Burton's full time teammate in WC and contended for the Raybestos Rookie-of-the-Year title against such highly touted talent as Matt Kenseth and Dale Earnhardt Jr. Blaney finished third in the 2000 rookie title chase.

Blaney's credentials include his superstar status in the highly competitive World of Outlaws (WoO) winged-sprint-car series. Ohioan Blaney was a constant nemesis to Mark and Steve Kinser for the series title. Blaney was the WoO champ in 1995 and finished second to Steve Kinser in 1993, 1994, 1996, and 1997.

Bill Davis recognized Blaney's considerable talents, putting him in a competitive racecar for 20 races in 1998. Blaney took full advantage in the audition season, was strong in qualifying, and had a few good finishes. The 1998 poles came at Georgia, Texas, Colorado, and Michigan tracks.

For the 2000 season, Blaney raced to a 31st-place finish in points standings. A strong late season charge saw Blaney

103

NASCAR DIECAST AND MODEL CARS

Today diecast models of Ward Burton's rides are plentiful both in the mass-market and collectibles market.

The Ertl Pro Shop diecast series features attractive packaging including these boxes for the No. 22 Ward Burton CAT Pontiac.

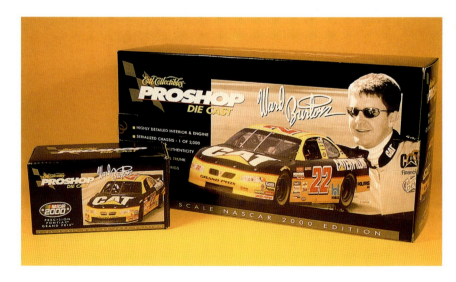

NASCAR DIECAST AND MODEL CARS

The Ertl Authentics series is the top of the line for this diecast manufacturer. The 1/24th-scale 2000 Amoco Ultimate No. 93 Pontiac features all the bells and whistles. Included with this high-quality piece is the inspection template, hydraulic jack, removable wheels, and exceptional engine and chassis detail. Note the display base nd clear cases that are included.

Here's a pair of Ertl Pro Shop No. 93 Amoco Pontiacs as driven by Dave Blaney for Bill Davis in 1/18th scale (rear) and 1/24th scale (front).

register a third place in the rookie title chase just 41 points behind Earnhardt Jr., who finished second to Matt Kenseth.

Introduction to Collectibles

Since becoming an active participant in stock car racing, Bill Davis has been associated with drivers such as Mark Martin, Jeff Gordon, and Bobby Labonte. Without a doubt, Davis today is most identified with his role as team owner for Ward Burton and Dave Blaney.

A few selected pieces of diecast exist that were created in the mid-1990s of Ward Burton's earlier BGN and WC rides. The model kit builder and collector had to wait until 2000 when Revell introduced a 1/24th-scale full-glue kit of the No. 22 CAT Pontiac Grand Prix.

Dave Blaney fans will find that collectibles are a bit on the sparse side. Racing Champions Ertl makes an excellent 1/24th-scale replica of the 2000 No. 93 Ultimate Pontiac in their premier Authentics line. At this writing, there are no plastic model kits of Dave Blaney's current ride or aftermarket decals.

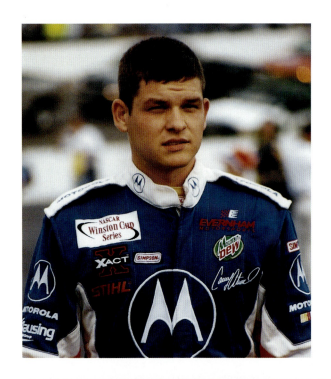

Above, left: *Young Casey Atwood was snapped up by Ray Evernham to drive the No. 19 Dodge for the 2001 season.*

Above, right: *Bill Elliott scored his lone championship title in 1988 at the wheel of the Coors No. 9 Thunderbird.*

Right: *Mike Madlinger built this 1989 Coors T-Bird using a Monogram 1/24th-scale kit and the decals from an AMT 1989 Coors kit.*

12

Evernham Motorsports

Ray Evernham

At the beginning of the 1999 season, it looked like business as usual at Hendrick Motorsports. Jeff Gordon and Ray Evernham had just won their second Daytona 500. As the new season labored on, the rumor mill was rife with talk of friction and disharmony with the No. 24 Hendrick machine's inner workings.

Finally, by September, Evernham announced his departure from the Hendrick operation to spearhead the return of Dodge to the NASCAR Winston Cup (WC) series. The rumors about his leaving to work for Dodge may have been partly responsible for the team's poor showing. There were nine finishes outside the top ten during the 1999 season. Included in those stats were seven DNFs. These are events that usually spell disaster. With new crew chief Brian Whitesell on board, the Dupont team quickly recorded two wins in a row at Martinsville and Charlotte, but it was too late. Some observers claim that Evernham's style and influence had been a pivotal element in the equation because the team struggled after his departure.

The New Jersey native came from a background in NASCAR modified racing and had considerable International Race of Champions (IROC) series tenure. Evernham joined up with Jeff Gordon at the Bill Davis operation to compete in Busch Grand National (BGN). When Gordon made the jump to Hendrick Motorsports in late 1992, Evernham was the natural choice to call the shots from behind the pit wall for the youthful phenom.

After nearly seven years of unqualified success with Hendrick Motorsports, Evernham was wisked away from the team and Chevrolet. The lure of even greater success in uncharted waters and a new challenge with Dodge was too good to pass up. This move also allowed Evernham to realize his dream of being a team owner.

In September 1999, Evernham announced that Dodge would return to NASCAR WC competition for the 2001 season. He has lead the development of a NASCAR-approved racing Dodge Intrepid. He spearheaded the development of a brand-new pushrod Dodge V-8 racing engine. Evernham is the key link fostering a new level of cooperation between individual teams competing in Dodges in 2001.

Evernham Motorsports merged with the Elliott operation in Georgia and North Carolina. Evernham's new partner, Bill Elliott, assumed the lead driver role for the new team. Sharing driver's chores with Elliott will be 19-year-old future superstar Casey Atwood, who is the youngest competitor to ever compete in the BGN series.

Bill Elliott

Bill Elliott had one great accomplishment in 2000 in spite of all the struggles and disappointments of the last few NASCAR WC seasons. Just when it looked like Elliott would permanently slip into back-marker status, Ray Evernham and Dodge threw him a very welcome lifeline. Elliott accepted the driving duties for the new No. 9 Evernham Motorsports Dodge for 2001. The 25-year travail of Elliott's considerable driving skills and potent Ford racecars ended with the 2000 season.

In 1976, when the Elliott clan broke into the racing business, it was to field a family-owned Ford for "Million Dollar" Bill. Brothers Ernie and Dan, along with their soon-to-be-famous sibling, constructed, tuned, and set up racecars. Bill and family arrived at a sterling moment for Ford. The manufacturer had been out of racing since mid-1972, and frankly their racecars weren't that competitive. Bill and his family of dedicated racers revived Ford's presence in

NASCAR DIECAST AND MODEL CARS

This is a pair of Budweiser No. 11 T-Birds that Bill Elliott drove for former driving great Junior Johnson in 1992. Daryl Huhtala built the 1/25th-scale version on the left using a modified AMT kit and aftermarket decals. Len Carsner built the 1/32nd-scale version on the right from a Monogram kit and aftermarket decals.

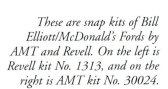

These are snap kits of Bill Elliott/McDonald's Fords by AMT and Revell. On the left is Revell kit No. 1313, and on the right is AMT kit No. 30024.

NASCAR, and over the next decade, made the marque a solid contender.

Since those humble beginnings, Bill has risen to major superstar status in NASCAR racing. He had his first victory in 1983 at Riverside Raceway in California. He recorded 11 victories in 1985, and he nearly won his first WC championship. Bill set the all-time qualifying record of over 212 miles per hour at Talledega in 1988. Bill has 40 wins and 49 poles to his credit. He was the first driver to win the Winston Million. Bill won the WC championship in 1988 and has dominated the "Most Popular Driver" balloting for all but 2 of the past 17 years. In 2000, Elliott garnered more than twice the votes of his closest rival, Dale Earnhardt, in again being chosen by the fans as their favorite driver.

Casey Atwood

Antioch, Tennessee, native Casey Atwood is touted as one of the brightest future stars in NASCAR racing. At 17,

NASCAR DIECAST AND MODEL CARS

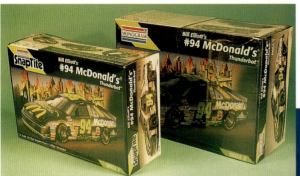

Monogram produced this pair of Bill Elliott/McDonald's Thunder Bat Thunderbirds in two scales to commemorate the motion picture Batman Forever. *Front: 1995 kit No. 1701; Rear: 1995 kit No. 2495.*

Shown are three Bill Elliott/McDonald's Fords in different scales. Counterclockwise: A Racing Champions 1/43rd-scale "Drive Thru" 1999 "Under-the-Lights" special paint scheme was used in six night races that season. A 1/24th-scale 1997 "Mac Tonite" Elliott Ford Thunderbird by Action Performance was run in five events that year. A 1/64th-scale 1999 Elliott "Drive Thru" Ford Taurus "regular" paint scheme, which is part of the Originals blister-pack series by Racing Champions.

he was the youngest driver ever to compete in the NASCAR BGN series. Atwood made his mark there during the 1999 season. With his wins in the Diehard 250 at the Milwaukee Mile and Dover Downs, Atwood became the youngest winner in the history of the series.

Atwood, like so many of the current crop of professional drivers, started out racing go-karts at age 10. From there, he moved up to four-cylinder cars at 14, and then on to the Late Model Sportsman stock cars at 15. He went on to win more than a dozen races that season at the tracks near his Tennessee home. Remember that all of these accomplishments were achieved by Atwood before he qualified for a driver's license.

Atwood will pilot the No. 19 Dodge Intrepid during the 2001 season for Evernham Motorsports. Can Ray Evernham and Casey Atwood become the new Evernham/Gordon of the new millennium? We'll just have to wait and see!

NASCAR DIECAST AND MODEL CARS

A 1/24th-scale No. 27 Castrol Monte Carlo and a 1/64th-scale New Stars of NASCAR series No. 27 Chevy are two more examples of Casey Atwood collectibles from the Hasbro Winner's Circle.

NASCAR DIECAST AND MODEL CARS

Action Performance made this 1/64th-scale diecast with removable body and 1/24th-scale replicas of the No. 19 Dodge Intrepids before Ray Evernham announced his choice of drivers for the 2001 season.

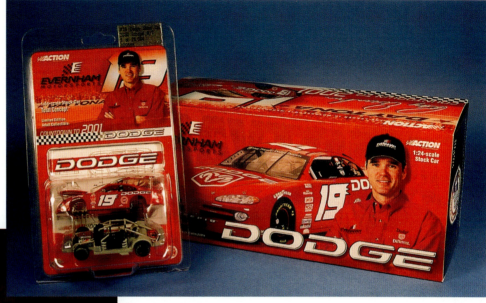

Hasbro Winner's Circle produced mass-market diecast items representing Chevrolet Monte Carlos driven by Casey Atwood in 2000. A 1/64th-scale New Stars of NASCAR series No. 27 Chevy (left) and a 1/24th-scale No. 27 Castrol Monte Carlo (right) are shown.

Introduction to Collectibles

In 2000, Evernham Motorsports absorbed the assets of Bill Elliott's operation in Georgia and North Carolina. As team owner, Evernham will call the shots for the new No. 9 Dodge driven by Bill Elliott and field the new No. 19 Dodge Intrepid, which has Busch series star Casey Atwood at the wheel.

For purposes of organization and clarity, a brief history of Bill Elliott's illustrious career is told through diecast models and plastic kits under Evernham Motorsports. What is shown here is but a few of the many different items included among a comprehensive list of Elliott collectibles.

Casey Atwood as the "new kid on the block" currently suffers from a lack of collectible items. With some measure of success on the racetrack in the coming new season and with the publicity that will understandably come with Dodge's re-entry into the sport, we should see many new diecast models and plastic kits available for this promising driver.

111

Mike Madlinger built this pair of 1987 and 1989 (front) Alan Kulwicki Zerex Ford Thunderbirds from Monogram 1/24th-scale kits and aftermarket decals.

Daryl Huhtala built the 1988 1/24th-scale version of Kulwicki's Zerex Thunderbird from a Monogram kit and JNJ decals. I built the 1/43rd-scale 1987 scale version on the right from a Starter kit to commemorate his first WC victory that season at Phoenix.

Operating on a shoestring budget, Wisconsin native Alan Kulwicki won the NASCAR Rookie-of-the-Year title in 1986. By 1992, Kulwicki was the national champion.

13

Alan Kulwicki Racing

Alan Kulwicki

Alan Kulwicki could be described as the ultimate "hard luck kid." As a child, Kulwicki experienced a tough life. Losing his mother when he was in the second grade was the first blow. His grandmother took over the job of raising him, and five years later she was also gone. One year later, he lost a brother. Rather than throw in the towel, these experiences hardened young Kulwicki's resolve and fostered his profound self-reliance.

Kulwicki and his father, Jerry, lived in Greenfield, a suburb of Milwaukee, Wisconsin. Jerry was a respected racecar engine builder on the United States Auto Club (USAC) stock car circuit. Alan observed his father's skills and work ethic with great interest, and learned important life lessons. Jerry insisted that Alan, his surviving son, bypass the racing business and become a college graduate. Alan wasn't able to completely turn his back on racing, though.

While working toward a mechanical engineering degree from the University of Wisconsin-Milwaukee, Alan worked and raced part-time on Wisconsin short tracks. Jerry couldn't ignore his son's budding talents any longer and realized that Alan could really prepare and drive a stock car. After graduation in 1977, Kulwicki took a job with Bear Alignment to occasionally provide technical expertise during the month of May at the Indianapolis Motor Speedway.

Kulwicki took his racing fetish on to the American Speed Association (ASA) and became a fixture on the circuit. His greatest accomplishment was winning the 1983 Miller 200 at the Wisconsin State Fairgrounds' Milwaukee Mile.

After the 1985 ASA season, Alan felt the lure of NASCAR's lucrative Winston Cup (WC) circuit. Selling off all his racing equipment and loading everything else he had into an old pickup truck, Alan headed for Greenville, South Carolina. He was firmly convinced that he could make a living racing in the highly competitive series. Alan also positioned himself for the 1986 season to compete for the Rookie-of-the-Year honors.

Kulwicki convinced the Quincy's Steak House chain to sponsor his borrowed Ford Thunderbird for one event. He was unable to qualify for the Daytona 500, but he was somehow able to persuade the restaurant operation to provide the finances to allow him to compete in 15 races in 1986. Alan was the highest finishing rookie in 18 of 23 events in 1986 and edged out Michael Waltrip to take the rookie title.

Over the next few seasons, Alan rigidly maintained his own bare-bones operation. For the 1987 season, Alan's 'Birds carried the Zerex antifreeze livery. During this stint, Alan scored his very first WC victory at Phoenix International Raceway. Attempting to make his post-race celebration unique, Alan made a clockwise lap of the track. Thus was born the famous "Polish Victory Lap."

Alan succeeded in landing a sponsorship for the 1992 WC season from the Hooters restaurant chain. In the closest finish in series history, Alan captured the championship by 10 points over runners-up Bill Elliott and Davey Allison.

Kulwicki had very little opportunity to revel in his accomplishments. The 1992 NASCAR WC champion was killed in a plane crash near Blountsville, Tennessee, April 1, 1993. He sadly joins the ranks of a growing list of promising and seasoned drivers who lost their lives pursuing their dreams: Davey Allison, Neil Bonnett, Adam Petty, and Kenny Irwin. Kulwicki has one distinction separating him from fellow fallen comrades as well as those who survived him: He achieved his primary goal and won the NASCAR WC championship. His achievement is all the sweeter because he did it his way, on his terms, and on a shoestring budget!

NASCAR DIECAST AND MODEL CARS

Above: *Daryl Huhtala built these 1/24th-scale replicas of Kulwicki's racecars. The kit on the left was built from a Monogram 1989 Zerex kit, and the kit on the right is the army paint scheme used for the 1991 Daytona 500 using a Monogram kit and JNJ decals.*

Left: *A Buck Fever (Monogram tooling) Hooter's No. 7 kit (No. 0762), and a Monogram Zerex No. 7 kit (No. 2908) are two 1/24th-scale collectibles of Alan Kulwicki kits.*

Introduction to Collectibles

Many Kulwicki collectible items seen today were released after his death. The first Kulwicki collectibles were 1/25th- and 1/24th-scale plastic kits from AMT and Revell-Monogram. Both companies produced kits of the 1989 Zerex No. 7 Fords campaigned by Alan.

At the time of his death, kit manufacturers and after-market decal makers such as SLIXX were on the verge of releasing a product that represented his championship Ford Thunderbird. Eventually, plastic kits and diecast cars were offered by a variety of manufacturers and in many scales. The French company Starter produced a very limited number of Kulwicki racecars in 1/43rd-scale resin kits.

For a brief period after Kulwicki's death, his collectibles shot up dramatically in value as a few speculators tried to make some extra loot. A few new products have been released lately, and the value of existing items has stabilized.

NASCAR DIECAST AND MODEL KITS VALUE GUIDE

Above: These two 1/24th-scale built models showcase the career of the late Alan Kulwicki. I built the 1986 Quincy's No. 35 rookie car using a Monogram kit and JNJ decals. Mike Madlinger built this 1992 championship Hooter's No. 7 using a Monogram kit and aftermarket decals.

Right: A Racing Champions 1993 1/43rd-scale diecast Alan Kulwicki Pit Stop Show Case is on the left, and a Quartzo 1/43rd-scale diecast of Kulwicki's 1992 championship Thunderbird is on the right.

NASCAR DIECAST and MODEL KIT **VALUE GUIDE**

The following data constitutes a Value Guide for NASCAR diecast and plastic model kits in this book. Much of this information is taken from the pages of The Directory of Model Car Kits by Bob Shelton and Bill Coulter, Stock Car Model Kit Encyclopedia and Price Guide by Bill Coulter as well as monthly periodicals like Beckett Racing & Motorsports Marketplace and Racing Collector's Price Guide.

Again, be aware that asking prices for any of the items shown in this book can vary widely depending on condition, availability, and demand. Often after the untimely and tragic death of a driver, prices may "go through the roof" for a while, and availability is also a critical determining factor. Remember, the actual final sale price of any racing collectible item is that to which seller and buyer agree on and product and money change hands.

CHAPTER 1

Revell Collection	.98 28 Havoline Taurus	1/18th	$130
Action Performance	.98 28 Havoline Taurus	1/24th	$90
Revell Collection	.98 28 Havoline Taurus	1/43rd	$35
Hasbro Winner's Circle	.98 28 Havoline Taurus	1/64th	$20
Monogram 2939	.90 30 Pennzoil Pontiac GP	1/24th kit	$15
Ertl	.97 30 Pennzoil Pontiac GP	1/18th	$30
Revell Collection	.96 30 Pennzoil Pontiac GP	1/24th	$29
Revell Collection	.97 30 Pennzoil Pontiac GP	1/43rd	$20
Revell Collection	.97 30 Pennzoil Pontiac GP	1/64th	$7
Racing Champions	.97 30 Pennzoil Pontiac GP	1/144th	$3
Revell Collection	.97 35 Tabasco Pontiac GP	1/18th	$70
Revell Collection	.97 35 Tabasco Pontiac GP	1/24th	$45
Monogram 4129	.97 35 Tabasco Pontiac GP	1/24th kit	$15
Hot Wheels	.98 35 Tabasco Pontiac GP	1/43rd	$10
Revell Collection	.97 35 Tabasco Transporter	1/64th	$20
Revell Collection	.97 35 Tabasco Pontiac GP	1/64th	$10 (3 versions)
Revell Collection	.97 40 Coors Lite Chevrolet MC	1/18th	$65
Revell Collection	.97 33 Skoal Chevrolet MC	1/18th	$90
Action Performance	.99 31 Gargoyles Chevrolet MC	1/24th	$115

116

NASCAR DIECAST AND MODEL KITS VALUE GUIDE

CHAPTER 2

Team Caliber	.99 43 STP Pontiac GP	1/24th	$100
AMT	.90 43 STP Pontiac GP	1/25th kit	$30
AMT	.93 43 STP Pontiac GP	1/25th kit	$25
Ertl	92 6 Valvoline T-Bird	1/18th	$50
Ertl	.81 Buick Regal 4-car set	1/64th	$100
Hasbro Winner's Circ	.98 28 Havoline Taurus	1/24th	$40
Hasbro Winner's Circle	.98 28 Havoline Taurus	1/43rd	$25
Hasbro Winner's Circle	.98 28 Havoline Taurus	1/64th	$20
Hasbro Pit Row	.98 28 car/crew/pit scene	1/64th	$25
Petty Fathers' Day	.98 43, 44, 45 racecars	1/64th	$60
Petty Generations	.98 42, 43, 44 racecars	1/64th	$35
Petty Team/Players	.98 43, 44, 43 CTS Dodge	1/64th	$15
Petty 50th Anniversary	.99 43, 44, 45 cars, 43 CTS	1/64th ...(WalMart exclusive)	$50
Monogram 2492	.97 97 John Deere Pontiac GP	1/24th kit	$12
Action Performance	.98 1 Coca-Cola MC/Japan	1/24th	$100
Action Performance	.98 3 Coca-Cola MC/Japan	1/24th	$200
Racing Champions	.98 Petty 7 title cars/Trans	1/64th	$60

CHAPTER 4

Hot Wheels	.98 43 50th Anniversary Pontiac	1/24th	$100
Hot Wheels	.98 44 50th Anniversary Pontiac	1/24th	$100
Hot Wheels	.98 45 50th Anniversary Chevrolet MC	1/24th	$150
Franklin Mint	.70 43 Plym. Superbird	1/24th	$125
Franklin Mint	.67 43 Plymouth GTX	1/24th	$125
Racing Champions	.50 42 Plymouth	1/64th	$30
Racing Champions	.53 42 Dodge	1/64th	$30
Racing Champions	.55 42 Chrysler C-300	1/64th	$25
Ertl	.77 43 STP Chevrolet MC	1/25th	$100

117

NASCAR DIECAST AND MODEL CARS

CHAPTER 4

Ertl	.81 43 STP Buick Regal	1/43rd	$200
Monogram 2722	.85 43 STP Pontiac GP	1/24th kit	$100
Monogram 3151	.84 43 STP/200th Victory	1/24th kit	$15
Hot Wheels	.98 44 HW/Blues Brothers 2000	1/24th	$30
Action Performance	.96 44 Hot Wheels Protest	1/24th	$100
Racing Champions	.99 43 Thank You F. F. PGP	1/24th	$100
Action Performance	.96 43 STP 25th Anniversary PGP	1/24th	$150
Racing Champions	.94 43 Black Flag/Frenchs PGP	1/24th	$75
Team Caliber	.99 45 Spree Chevrolet MC	1/24th	$200
Team Caliber	.00 45 Sprint Chevrolet MC	1/24th	$200
Revell-Monogram kit	.99 44 HW/Charity Ride	1/24th	$150 (built)
Revell-Monogram kit	.97 44 HW/500th Start	1/24th	$150 (built)

CHAPTER 5

Revell-Monogram 2525	.97 24 Jurassic Park MC	1/24th kit	$25
Revell-Monogram 2476	.96 24 Dupont Chevrolet MC	1/24th kit	$20
Hasbro Gar. Scn.	.99 24 Dupont car/two figures	1/43rd	$15
Revell Collection	.99 24 Superman Chevrolet MC	1/24th	$120
Hasbro Winner's Circle	.99 24 Dupont Chevrolet MC	1/43rd	$12
Revell Collection	.98 24 Chromalusion MC	1/64th	$25
Racing Champions	.96 24 Dupont Chevrolet MC	1/144th	$25
Monogram 2755	.87 17 Tide Chevrolet MC	1/24th kit	$95 (unbuilt)
Monogram 2755	.87 17 Tide Chevrolet MC	1/24th kit	$150 (built)
Monogram kit	.87 17 Tide 89 Daytona Winner	1/24th	$150 (built)
Monogram kit	.90 17 Chev. Lumina	1/24th	$150 (built)
Monogram kit	.87 35 Folgers Chevrolet MC	1/24th	$150 (built)
Starter kit	.87 25 Folgers Chevrolet MC	1/43rd	$150 (built)
Revell Select	.97 25 Louie the Lizard MC	1/24th	$70
Revell Collection	.97 25 Budweiser Chevrolet MC	1/43rd	$25

NASCAR DIECAST AND MODEL KITS VALUE GUIDE

CHAPTER 5

Racing Champions	.97 25 "Ricky" Chevrolet MC	1/144th	$5
Revell Collection	.00 25 Coast Guard MC	1/24th	$ 60 (Bank set)
Revell Collection	.00 25 Coast Guard MC	1/64th	$ 15 (Bank Set)
Revell Collection	.97 5 Tony the Tiger	1/24th	$220
Revell Collection	.97 5 Tony the Tiger	1/43rd	$35
Team Caliber	.00 5 Kellogg's Chevrolet MC	1/24th	$85
Revell Collection	.98 5 Tony the Tiger MC	1/43rd	$30
Hasbro Winner's Circle	.99 5 Kellogg's Chevrolet MC	1/64th	$12
Racing Champions	.97 5 Kellogg's Chevrolet MC	1/144th	$5
Testors 7132	.98 5 Kellogg's Chevrolet MC	1/24th kit	$15
Racing Champions	.00 5 Kellogg's Chevrolet MC	1/64th	$12

CHAPTER 6

Hasbro Winner's Circle	.79 2 Wrangler Chevrolet MC	1/64th	$15
Hasbro Winner's Circle	.86 3 Wrangler Chevrolet MC	1/64th	$15
Hasbro Winner's Circle	.00 3 Goodwrench Chevrolet MC	1/64th	$15
Ertl	.81 15 Wrangler T-Bird	1/64th	$250
Revell Collection	.96 3 Olympic Chev. MC	1/64th	$25
Monogram 6298	.81/86 2/3 Wrangler GP/MC	1/24th kit	$100
Action Performance	.86/87 Wrangler Trans.	1/64th	$300
Action Performance	.86/87 Wrangler Trans.	1/96th	$250
Starter kit	.87 3 Wrangler Chevrolet MC	1/43rd	$250 (built)
Starter kit	.88 3 Goodwrench Chevrolet MC	1/43rd	$250 (built)
Starter kit	.91 3 Goodwrench Lumina	1/43rd	$250 (built)
Action Perfromance	.96 3 Olympics Chevrolet MC	1/24th	$150
Action Performance	.97 3 Winston 25th Anniversary	1/24th	$150
Action Performance	.97 3 Wheaties Chevrolet MC	1/24th	$300
Action Performance	.00 3 Peter Max Chevrolet MC	1/24th	$350
Revell-Monogram 2523	.97 31 Lowes Chevrolet MC	1/24th kit	$15

119

NASCAR DIECAST AND MODEL CARS

CHAPTER 6

Revell-Monogram 85-2991	.00 31 Lowes Chevrolet MC	1/24th kit	$12
Action Performance	.98 31 Lowes Chevrolet MC	1/24th	$50
Action Performance	.98 31 Special Olympics MC	1/24th	$60
Revell Collection	.98 31 Special Olympics MC	1/24th	$100
Revell Collection	.98 31 Special Olympics MC	1/43rd	$30
Action Performance	.98 1 Pennzoil/1st Brickyard	1/24th	$150
Hasbro Winner's Circle	.99 1 Pennzoil Chevrolet MC	1/43rd	$12
Hasbro Winner's Circle	.99 1 Pennzoil Chevrolet MC	1/64th	$8
Action Performance	.96/7 31 Gargoyles MC	1/24th	$125
Action Performance	.96/7 31 Mom 'n' Pops MC	1/24th	$140
Action Performance	.99 8 U.S. Olympics MC	1/24th	$190
Action Performance	.99 8 Budweiser Chevrolet MC	1/24th	$150
Hasbro WC Vic. Cel.	.98 3 Delco car/two figures	1/43rd	$50
Revell Collection	.98 3 Delco Chevrolet MC	1/24th	$150
Revell Collection	.98 3 Delco Chevrolet MC	1/43rd	$35
Hasbro Winner's Circle	.98 3 Delco Chevrolet MC	1/64th	$20

CHAPTER 7

Monogram kit	.83 28 Hardee's Chev. MC	1/24th	$200 (built)
Starter kit	.85 28 Hardee's T-Bird	1/43rd	$150 (built)
Starter kit	.87 28 Havoline T-Bird	1/43rd	$70 (unbuilt)
Starter kit	.87 28 Havoline T-Bird	1/43rd	$200 (built)
Revell 85-2990	.87 28 Havoline T-Bird	1/24th kit	$15 (unbuilt)
Revell 85-2990	.87 28 Havoline T-Bird	1/24th kit	$150 (built)
Monogram kit	.87 2 Krogers/Pepsi MC	1/24th	$200 (built)
Monogram kit	.91 4 Kodak Chev. Lumina	1/24th	$200 (built)
Monogram 6367	.91/86 Kodak Chev./Oldsmobile	1/24th kit	$30
Revell Collection	.98 28 Havoline T-Bird	1/18th	$100
Revell Collection	.98 28 Havoline T-Bird	1/64th	$25

NASCAR DIECAST AND MODEL KITS VALUE GUIDE

CHAPTER 7

Action Performance	.98 88 Batman Taurus	1/24th	$125
Revell Collection	.98 28 Joker Taurus	1/24th	$60
Monogram kit	.89 26 Quaker State Buick	1/24th`	$150 (built)
Starter kit	.89 26 Quaker State Buick	1/43rd	$150 (built)
Action Performance	.00 28 Havoline Taurus	1/24th	$60
Revell Collection	.00 28 Marines Taurus	1/24th	$67
Hasbro Winner's Circle	.98 88 QC/Winston Million	1/43rd	$25
Hasbro Winner's Circle	.00 88 Daytona 500 Vic.	1/43rd	$25
Revell-Monogram 2472	.96 88 Quality Care T-Bird	1/24th kit	$18
Revell-Monogram kit	.96 88 Quality Care T-Bird	1/24th	$150 (built)
Action Performance	.98 88 Batman Taurus	1/24th	$85
Revell Collection	.98 88 Batman Taurus	1/43rd	$30

CHAPTER 8

RMonogram kit	.90 6 Folgers T-Bird	1/24th	$150 (built)
Starter kit	.90 6 Folgers T-Bird	1/43rd	$150 (built)
Monogram 2477	.96 Valvoline T-Bird	1/24th	$18 (unbuilt)
Monogram kit	.96 Valvoline T-Bird	1/24th	$150 (built)
Revell Collection	.97 6 Valvoline T-Bird	1/18th	$75
Revell Collection	.97 60 Wynn-Dixie BGN	1/18th	$75
Team Caliber	.00 6 Eagle One T-Bird	1/24th	$100
Team Caliber	.99 6 Valvoline T-Bird	1/64th	$20
Revell Collection	.97 99 Exide T-Bird	1/43rd	$55
Team Caliber	.98 99 Exide Taurus	1/64th	$18
Racing Champions	.96 99 Exide T-Bird	1/144th	$4
Monogram kit	.95 8 Raybestos T-Bird	1/24th	$150 (built)
Monogram kit	.97 99 Exide T-Bird	1/24th	$150 (built)
Revell 1314	.99 99 Exide Taurus	1/24th kit	$15

121

NASCAR DIECAST AND MODEL CARS

CHAPTER 8

Revell 2558	.99 99 Exide Taurus	1/24th kit	$20
Racing Champions	.00 17 DeWalt Taurus	1/64th	$9
Hot Wheels	.99 17 DeWalt Taurus	1/64th	$9
Team Caliber	.99 17 DeWalt Taurus	1/24th	$165
Team Caliber	.99 17 DeWalt BGN Chev. MC	1/24th	$125
Team Caliber	.00 17 DeWalt Taurus	1/24th	$85
Team Caliber	.00 16 Familyclick.com Tar.	1/24th	$65
Hot Wheels	.98 16 Primestar Taurus	1/64th	$5
Revell Collection	.97 97 John Deere Pontiac GP	1/43rd	$40
Revell Select	.97 97 John Deere 160th Anniv. PGP	1/24th	$35
Revell-Monogram 2492	.97 97 John Deere Pontiac GP	1/24th kit	$20
Revell 85-1316	.98 26 Cheerios Taurus	1/24th kit	$12
Revell 2553	.98 26 Cheerios Taurus	1/24th	$15
Ertl	.97 30 Pennzoil Pontiac GP	1/18th	$35
Revell Collection	.96 30 Pennzoil Pontiac GP	1/24th	$35
Revell Collection	.97 30 Pennzoil Pontiac GP	1/43rd	$24
Racing Champions	.97 30 Pennzoil Pontiac GP	1/144th	$5

CHAPTER 9

HMonogram kit	.86 27 Alugard Pontiac GP	1/24th	$200 (built)
Starter kit	.86 27 Alugard Pontiac GP	1/43rd	$150 (built)
AMT 6961	.90 27 Miller Pontiac GP	1/25th	$50
Monogram 2960	.92 2 Pontiac Excitement	1/24th kit	$20
Revell Collection	.99 2 Adv. of Rusty Taurus	1/24th	$150
Revell Collection	.99 2 Miller Lite Taurus	1/24th	$60
Revell Collection	.00 2 Miller Lite Taurus	1/24th	$70
Revell Collection	.97 2 Miller Lite T-Bird	1/43rd	$40
Revell Collection	.98 2 Elvis/Miller Lite Tar.	1/64th	$15

NASCAR DIECAST AND MODEL KITS VALUE GUIDE

CHAPTER 9

GMP (Ertl)	.97 37 Kmart/RC Cola T-B	1/18th	$70
Revell Collection	.97 37 Kmart /RC Cola T-B	1/24th	$45
Hasbro Winner's Circle	.97 37 Kmart /RC Cola T-B	1/43rd	$15
Racing Champions	.97 37 Kmart /RC Cola T-B	1/144th	$4
Team Caliber	.99 12 Mobil 1 Taurus	1/24th	$80
Revell Collection	.99 12 Mobil 1 Taurus	1/43rd	$25

CHAPTER 10

Revell kit	.99 20 Home Depot Pontiac GP	1/24th	$150 (built)
Revell 1646	.99 20 Home Depot Pontiac GP	1/24th kit	$15 (unbuilt)
Action Performance	.99 20 Habitat for Humanity PGP	1/18th	$150
Revell Collection	.99 20 R-O-T-Y Pontiac GP	1/24th	$225
Hasbro Winner's Circle	.99 20 Home Depot Pontiac GP	1/43rd	$25
Hasbro New Stars	.99 20 Home Depot Pontiac GP	1/64th	$10
Revell Collection	.99 20 R-O-T-Y Pontiac GP	1/24th	$225
Revell kit	.99 20 Home Depot Pontiac GP	1/24th	$150 (built)
Ertl	.95 18 Interstate Battery Chevrolet MC	1/18th	$40
Action Performance	92 18 Interstate Battery Chevrolet Lumina	1/24th	$55
Ertl	.95 18 Interstate Battery Chevrolet MC	1/18th	$40
Revell Collection	.97 18 Texas WS Pontiac GP	1/18th	$100
Revell Collection	.98 18 Hot Rod magazine Pontiac GP	1/24th	$110
Revell Collection	.99 18 Small Soldiers Pontiac GP	1/43rd	$35
Hasbro's Winner's Circle	00 18 Interstate Battery Pontiac GP	1/43rd	$15

123

NASCAR DIECAST AND MODEL CARS

CHAPTER 11

RRacing Champions	.92 2 Hardee's Chev. Lumina	1/24th	$55
Racing Champions	.95 31 Hardee's Chev. Lumina	1/24th	$50
Racing Champions	.96 22 Maxwell House Pontiac GP	1/24th	$50
Action Performance	.99 22 CAT Pontiac GP	1/24th	$140
Hot Wheels	.99 22 CAT Pontiac GP	1/24th	$40
Hasbro	.99 22 CAT Pontiac GP	1/24th	$20
Racing Champions	.99 22 CAT Pontiac GP	1/24th	$18
Revell 85-2992	.99 22 CAT Pontiac GP	1/24th kit	$18
Racing Champions	.99 22 CAT Pontiac GP	1/64th kit	$8
Ertl Authentics	.00 93 Am. Ult. Pontiac GP	1/24th	$75
Ertl Pro Shop	.00 93 Am. Ult. Pontiac GP	1/18th	$80
Ertl Pro Shop	.00 93 Am. Ult. Pontiac GP	1/24th	$35

CHAPTER 12

HMonogram kit	.89 9 Coors Thunderbird	1/24th	$200 (built)
AMT kit	.92 9 Budweiser T-Bird	1/25th	$100 (built)
AMT kit	.92 9 Budweiser T-Bird	1/32nd	$25 (built)
Revell-Monogram 1313	.99 94 McDonalds Taurus	1/24th kit	$15
AMT 30024	.99 94 McDonalds Taurus	1/25th kit	$12
Revell-Monogram 1701	.95 94 Thunderbat T-Bird	1/32th kit	$10
Revell-Monogram 2495	.95 94 Thunderbat T-Bird	1/24nd kit	$20
Racing Champions	.99 94 Un. the Lts. Taurus	1/43rd	$12
Action Performance	.97 94 Mac Tonite T-Bird	1/24th	$85
Racing Champions	.99 94 Drive Thru Taurus	1/64th	$10
Hasbro Winner's Circle	.00 27 Castrol Chev. MC	1/24th	$15
Hasbro Winner's Circle	.00 27 Castrol Chev. MC	1/64th	$5
Action Performance	.01 19 Dodge Intrepid	1/24th	$40
Action Performance	.01 19 Dodge Intrepid	1/64th	$10

NASCAR DIECAST AND MODEL KITS VALUE GUIDE

CHAPTER 13

RMonogram kit	.88 7 Zerex T-Bird	1/24th	$200 (built)
Starter kit	.88 7 Zerex T-Bird	1/43rd	$200 (built)
Monogram kit	.87 7 Zerex T-Bird	1/24th	$200 (built)
Monogram kit	.89 7 Zerex T-Bird	1/24th	$200 (built)
Buck Fever 0761	.92 7 Hooter's T-Bird	1/24th kit	$50
Monogram 2908	.89 7 Zerex T-Bird	1/24th kit	$80
Monogram kit	.89 7 Zerex Thunderbird	1/24th	$200 (built)
Monogram kit	.91 7 Army Thunderbird	1/24th	$200 (built)
Racing Champions	.93 7 Pit Stop Show Case	1/43rd	$100
Quartzo	.93 7 Hooter's T-Bird	1/43rd	$55
Monogram kit	.86 7 Quincy Steak House T-Bird	1/24th	$250 (built)
Monogram kit	.92 7 Hooter's Thunderbird	1/24th	$250 (built)

APPENDIX: SOURCES

Where to Buy Diecast Models, Plastic Kits, Etc. Today, it's possible to find NASCAR diecast and plastic kits in virtually any retail venue. Discount, general retail, drug, grocery, specialty, and collectibles stores sell these cars. Hobby shops, mail-order sources, model car flea markets and diecast swap meets, racing team merchandise trailers (at the racetracks), and QVC and HSN television shopping networks are also an outlet for these collectibles.

I am a satisfied customer of the following resellers:

Kalgin
Diecast Racecars
11057 W. Colonial Dr.
Ocoee, FL 34761
www.diecast-racecars.com

Preferred Line Motorsports, Inc.
3021 N. John Young Pkwy.
Orlando, FL 32804
www.preferredline.com

Winners Circle, Inc.
872 W. Main St.
Salem, VA 24153
or
2501 Williamson Rd.
Roanoke, VA 24012
www.winnerscircleinc.com

ThorTek
2800A West Main St.
League City, TX 77573
www.thortek.com

Southern Motorsports Hobbies
1111 Floral Drive

Lenoir, NC 28645
www.smhracing.com

BSR Replicas and Finishes
101 Rainbow Way
Fayetteville, GA 30214
www.BSRREP.com

Model Empire
7116 W. Greenfield Ave.
West Allis, WI 53214
www.modelempireusa.com

ModelMaxx
435 S Wesleyan Blvd.
Rocky Mount, NC 27803
1-800-948-8072

Lonestar Collectibles
8477 N. Frwy.
Houston, TX 77037
www.LoneStarFord.com

Model Roundup
443 The North Chace
Atlanta, GA 30328-4252

E-mail: roundup@mindspring.com

Treasure Coast Racing Collectibles
6841 S. U.S. Highway 1
Port St. Lucie, FL 34952
E-mail: nora.m.henderson@usa.com

Venture Hobbies
23 Huntington Ln.
Wheeling, IL 60090
847-537-8669
www.venturehobbies.com

Hobby Country
203 North Ridgewood Dr.
Sebring, FL 33870
863-382-2455
E-mail: hobco@strato.net

INDEX

Action Performance Elite Series, 15, 16
Action Performance, 19, 21, 26
Allison, Bobby, 63, 64, 85
Allison, Clifford, 64
Allison, Davey, 62-66, 71, 113
Allison, Judy, 64
Andretti, John, 34, 35, 37, 38
Andretti, Mario, 37
Andy Petree Racing, 49
Atwood, Casey, 106-111
Bahari Racing, 82
Baker, Buddy, 37
Baldwin, Tommy, 102
Beadle, Raymond, 86
Benson, Johnny, 12, 82, 83
Bernstein, Kenny, 70, 71
Besser, Jack, 23
Bettenhausen, Gary, 85
Bickle, Rich, 40
Biffle, Greg, 75, 80, 83
Bill Davis Racing, 44
Blaney, Dave, 100, 103, 105
Bodine, Geoff, 76
Bodine, Jeff, 43
Bonnett, Neil, 64, 68, 113
Bown, Chuck, 83
Burton, Jeff, 74, 77-79, 81, 96, 102, 103
Burton, Ward, 77, 100, 102-105
Busch, Kurt, 75, 83
Carsner, Lew, 108
Childress, Richard, 53, 54, 56, 70
Chung, Peter, 24
Combs, Rodney, 39
Craven, Ricky, 45, 48, 49
Dale Earnhardt Chevrolet, 60

Dallenbach, Wally Jr., 37, 49, 83
Davis, Bill, 93, 94, 101, 102, 105, 107
Days of Thunder, 47, 49
DiGard Racing, 63
Dilliard, A. G., 102
Dillon, Mike, 53
Dods, Bob, 24
Doebling, Wayne, 77, 78
Donohue, Mark, 85
Duncan, Randy, 27
Dunlevy, Junie, 43, 43
Earnhardt, Dale Jr, 54-56, 58-61, 79, 103, 105
Earnhardt, Dale, 19, 38, 43, 50, 52-57, 61, 64, 66, 71, 85, 93, 108
Earnhardt, Ralph, 53
Eidam, Ed, 26
Elliott, Bill, 14, 49, 63, 106-109, 111, 113
Elliott, Dan, 107
Elliott, Ernie, 107
Ertl, Fred Sr., 24
Ertl/AMT, 19-21, 22, 24, 25, 41, 50
Evernham, Ray, 44, 45, 107, 109, 111
Farmer, Red, 64
France, Bill Sr., 35
Fred Cady Design, 50, 81, 86
Gannon, Tom, 24
Gant, Harry, 76
Gapp, Wayne, 75
Georgia Marketing and Promotions, 21, 26
Gibbs, Joe, 63, 68, 93-96, 102
Gill, Andy, 25
Gill, Stan, 21, 25
Glaser, Lew, 25
Gordon, Jeff, 19, 43-46, 50, 67, 70, 94, 101, 103, 105, 107
Green, Jeff, 55, 59
Grissom, Steve, 40, 41
Haas, Carl, 88

Hagan, Billy, 37, 46, 93
Hamby, Roger, 43
Hamilton, Bobby, 37, 39
Hamilton, Pete, 37
Harvick, Kevin, 53
Hasbro Winner's Circle, 21, 22, 60, 72
Haseleu, Nathan, 75
Hassenfeld, Helal, 21
Hassenfeld, Henry, 21
Hendrick Management Corporation, 43
Hendrick, Rick, 43, 44, 46, 47, 49, 70, 93, 94
Hensley, Jimmy, 37, 40
Holigan, Michael, 44, 49
Hornaday, Ron, 54, 56
Hossfeld, Chuck, 75
Hot Rod, 99
Hot Wheels, 15, 23, 24, 36
Huhtala, Daryl, 65, 108, 114
Hyde, Harry, 43, 47, 49
Inman, Dale, 42
IRT Design, 27
Irvan, Ernie, 62, 63, 66-68, 72, 93
Irwin, Kenny, 58, 62, 64, 67, 69, 70, 72, 113
Jackson, Leo, 58
Jarrett, Dale, 45, 62, 63, 67-69, 71-73, 93-97
Jarrett, Ned, 67, 93
Joe Gibbs Racing, 68
Jo-Han, 41
Johnson, Bob, 23, 26
Johnson, Junior, 46, 53, 54, 94, 108
Kendall, Tommy, 75
Kenseth, Matt, 59, 74, 79, 83, 103, 105
Kinser, Mark, 103

Kinser, Steve, 103
Kranefuss, Michael, 37, 85
Kranefuss-Haas, 88, 90
Kulwicki, Alan, 63, 64, 112-115
Kulwicki, Jerry, 113
Labonte, Bob, 93
Labonte, Bobby, 92-97, 101-103, 105
Labonte, Terry, 42, 43, 45-47, 550, 51, 93, 94
LaJoie, Randy, 49, 102
Lapage, Kevin, 81, 83
Lewis, Suzi, 26
Little, Chad, 81
Long, Tom, 26
Loomis, Robbie, 46
Madlinger, Mike, 41, 47, 66, 71, 86, 106, 112, 115
Makar, Jimmy, 68, 93
Marcis, Dave, 85
Martin, Julian, 101
Martin, Mark, 8, 20, 74-78, 101, 103, 105
Matchbox/Lesney, 20, 24
Mattel, 23, 24, 26, 36
Max, Peter, 57
Mayfield, Jeremy, 84, 87-91
McReynolds, Larry, 53, 57
Meyer, Boyd, 24
Minichamps, 19
Model Products Corporation (MPC), 41, 90
Monogram Models, Inc., 23-25
Moore, Bud, 53, 54, 70
Moyer, Wayne, 48, 56, 65, 86
Musgrave, Ted, 81, 83
Nadeau, Jerry, 44, 49, 50
Negre, Ed, 53
Nelson, Dick, 25, 26
Nelson, Jan, 25

Odyssey Partners, 24, 25
Osterland, Rod, 53, 54
Panch, Marvin, 37
Park, Steve, 54-59, 61
Parrott, Todd, 68
Parsons, Benny, 42, 43, 48, 49, 80
Paschal, Jim, 37
Penske South, 88
Penske, Roger, 85, 86
Petrose, Mike, 13, 15
Petty Enterprises, 35, 41
Petty Museum, 35
Petty, Adam, 34-36, 64, 69, 113
Petty, Kyle, 24, 35-37, 38, 41
Petty, Lee, 35, 37, 67
Petty, Linda, 34, 35
Petty, Patti, 35
Petty, Richard, 34, 35, 37, 38, 40, 46, 54, 67
Pickard, Carl, 26
Racing Champions, Inc., 21, 24, 25, 27
Ranier, Harry, 63, 65
Reder, Bob, 23
Reiser, Robby, 79, 80
Revell Collection, 25-27, 98
Revell, Inc., 24-26
Revell-Monogram, Inc., 24, 41
Richmond, Tim, 42, 43, 47, 49, 50, 64
Robert Yates Racing, 93
Roush Corporation, 27
Roush Industries, 75
Roush Racing, 27
Roush, Jack, 75, 80, 81, 101
Rudd, Al, 70
Rudd, Ricky, 43, 53, 54, 63, 64, 70-72
Ruttman, Joe, 83
Sabates, Felix, 38
Scale breakdown, 17
Scalextric, 98
Schrader, Ken, 43, 44,

Sheppard, T. G., 43
Skinner, Mark, 53, 54, 56, 57
SLIXX, 41, 50, 81, 98, 114
Speed, Lake, 63
Sprague, Jack, 44
Stacy, J. D., 76
Stavola Brothers, 78
Stewart, Cliff, 86
Stewart, Tony, 92-96, 98
Team Caliber, 15, 26, 27
Team Menard, 96
Team Sabco, 14, 38, 63
Wagenhals, Fred, 19
Wallace, Rusty, 84-89
Waltrip, Darrell, 42, 43, 47, 50, 76
Waltrip, Michael, 12, 55, 56, 113
Whitesell, Brian, 46, 107
Wood Brothers, 68
Yarborough, Cale, 37, 54, 64, 65, 68, 88
Yates, Robert, 63, 65, 66, 68-70

Models
1996 No. 31 Mom 'n' Pops Monte Carlo, 60
1997 No. 31 Gargoyles Monte Carlo, 60
1998 No. 18 *Hot Rod* Pontiac, 99
1998 No. 28 Halvoline, 10
1999 No. 8 Budweiser Monte Carlo, 61
2000 No. 8 Budweiser Olympic Monte Carlo, 61

Action Performance
1992 No. 18 Interstate Batteries Lumina, 97
1996 No. 3 Goodwrench Monte Carlo, 57

1996 No. 43 STP Pontiac, 39
1997 No. 3 Goodwrench Monte Carlo, 57
1997 No. 3 Wheaties Monte Carlo, 57
1998 No. 28 Batman/Joker Ford, 70
1998 No. 31 Lowe's Chevy, 58
1998 No. 31 Pennzoil Monte Carlo, 59
1998 No. 31 Special Olympics Chevy, 58
1998 No. 88 Batman/Joker Ford, 73
1999 No. 22 CAT Pontiac, 103
1999 No. 94 McDonalds Drive Thru Taurus, 109
2000 No. 3 Goodwrench Monte Carlo, 57
2001 No. 19 Dodge Intrepid, 111
No. 20 Habitat for Humanity Pontiac, 95
No. 31 Gargoyles Chevy, 16

AMT
1992 No. 11 Budweiser T-Bird, 108
No. 27 Miller Geniune Draft, 88

Ertl
1980 No. 43 STP Caprice, 39
1981 No. 43 STP Buick, 39
1982 No. 15 Wrangler T-Bird, 55

INDEX

1995 No. 18 Interstate Batteries Monte Carlo, 97
1997 No. 30 Pennzoil Pontiac, 82
2000 No. 93 Amoco Ultimate Pontiac, 105
No. 18 Interstate Batteries Monte Carlo, 97
No. 22 CAT Pontiac, 104
No. 6 Valvoline T-Bird, 20
No. 93 Amoco Pontiac, 105

Franklin Mint
1967 No. 43 GTX, 36
1973 No. 43 Plymouth Superbird, 36

GMP 1997 No. 37 Kmart/RC cola T-Bird, 90

Hasbro Winner's Circle
1997 No. 37 Kmart/RC cola Ford, 90
1998 No. 3 Delco Monte Carlo, 61
1998 Pennzoil Monte Carlo, 59
1999 No. 22 CAT Pontiac, 103
1999 No. 24 Dupont Monte Carlo, 46
1999 No. 5 Kellogg's Chev, 51
1999 No. Home Depot Pontiac, 95
2000 No. 18 Interstate Batteries Pontiac, 99
2000 No. 27 Castrol Monte Carlo, 111
2000 No. 27 Monte Carlo, 111
No. 27 Castrol Monte Carlo, 110

Hot Wheels
1998 No. 42 Blues Brothers 2000 Pontiac, 38
1999 No. 17 DeWalt Taurus, 80
1999 No. 22 CAT Pontiac, 103
No. 16 Primestar Taurus, 81
No. 35 Tabasco Pontiac, 12

Mattel 1997 No. 44 Hot Wheels Pontiac, 24

Monogram
1983 No. 28 Hardee's Monte Carlo, 64
1985 No. 43 STP Grand Prix, 38
1986 No. 27 Alugard Pontiac, 86
1986 No. 35 Quincy's 115
1987 No. 7 Zerex T-Bird, 112
1989 No. 17 Tide Monte Carlo, 47
1989 No. 26 Quaker State Buick, 71
1989 No. 7 Zerex T-Bird, 112
1989 No. 7 Zerex, 114
1991 No. 2 Pepsi Monte Carlo, 66
1991 No. 4 Kodak Chevy, 66
1991 No. 4 Kodak combo kit, 67
1991 No. 7 Army, 114
1992 No. 11 Budweiser T-Bird, 108
1992 No. 7 Hooter's, 115
1995 No. 94 Monte CarloDonalds Thunder Bat T-Bird, 109
1996 No. 24 Dupont Chevy, 45
1996 No. 6 Valvoline, 77
1997 No. 99 Exide Ford, 78
No. 25 Folgers, 48
No. 27 Pontiac, 88
No. 3 Wrangler combo, 55
No. 7 Hooter's, 114
No. 7 Zerex, 114
No. 8 Raybestos T-Bird, 78
No. 30 Pennzoil Pontiac, 12
No. 36 Pontiac, 69

Racing Champions
1950 No. 42 Plymouth, 37
1953 No. 42 Dodge, 37
1955 No. 42 Chrysler, 37
1992 No. 2 Hardee's Lumina, 102
1992 No. 7 Quartzo T-Bird, 115
1993 No. 7 Alan Kulwicki Pit Stop, 115
1994 No. 43 French's/Black Flag Pontiac, 39
1995 No. 31 Hardee's Lumina, 102
1996 No. 22 Maxwell House Pontiac, 102
1996 No. 99 Exide T-Bird, 79
1997 No. 2 Miller Lite T-Bird, 89
1997 No. 30 Pennzoil Pontiac, 82
1997 No. 37 Kmart/RC cola Ford, 90
1997 No. 5 Kellogg's Chevy, 51
1997 No. 94 Monte CarloDonalds Mac Tonite T-Bird, 109
1997 No. 97 John Deere Pontiac, 83
1998 No. 2 Elvis Ford, 89
1999 No. 22 CAT Pontiac, 103
1999 No. 43 STP Pontiac, 39
2000 No. 17 DeWalt Taurus, 80
2000 No. 2 Miller Lite Ford, 89
2000 No. 5 Kellogg's Chevy, 50
No. 94 Monte CarloDonalds Drive Thru, 109
No. 94 Monte CarloDonalds T-Bird, 108

Revell
1988 No. 28 Havoline T-Bird, 65
1997 No. 44 Hot Wheels Pontiac, 41
1997 No. 99 Exide Ford, 79
1998 No. 26 Cheerios Taurus, 82
1999 No. 20 Home Depot Pontiac, 94
1999 No. 22 CAT Pontiac, 103
1999 No. 44 Hot Wheels Pontiac, 41
1997 No. 30 Pennzoil Pontiac, 82
1997 No. 37 Kmart/RC cola Ford, 90
1997 No. 5 Kellogg's Chevy, 51
1997 No. 94 Monte CarloDonalds Mac Tonite T-Bird, 109
1998 No. 2 Elvis Ford, 89
1999 No. 22 CAT Pontiac, 103
2000 No. 17 DeWalt Taurus, 80
2000 No. 2 Miller Lite Ford, 89
2000 No. 5 Kellogg's Chevy, 50
No. 94 Monte CarloDonalds Drive Thru, 109
No. 94 Monte CarloDonalds T-Bird, 108

Revell
1988 No. 28 Havoline T-Bird, 65
1997 No. 44 Hot Wheels Pontiac, 41
1997 No. 99 Exide Ford, 79
1998 No. 26 Cheerios Taurus, 82
1999 No. 20 Home Depot Pontiac, 94
1999 No. 22 CAT Pontiac, 103
1999 No. 44 Hot Wheels Pontiac, 41
2000 No. 31 Lowe's Chevy, 58
No. 99 Exide Ford, 78

Revell Collection
1984 No. 43 STP Grand Prix, 38
1994 No. 94 Monte CarloDonalds T-Bird, 108
1996 No. 3 Olympics Monte Carlo, 55
1996 No. 30 Pennzoil Pontiac, 82
1997 No. 18 Interstate Batteries Pontiac, 99
1997 No. 30 Pennzoil Pontiac, 82
1997 No. 6 Valvoline T-Bird, 8, 76
1997 No. 60 Winn-Dixie Ford, 8, 76
1998 No. 28 Batman/Joker Ford, 70
1998 No. 3 Delco Monte Carlo, 61
1998 No. 5 Tony the Tiger Chevy, 51
1998 No. 88 Batman/Joker Ford, 73
1999 No. 12 Mobil 1 Taurus, 91
1999 No. 20 Home Depot Pontiac, 96, 98
1999 No. 31 Lowe's Special Olympics Chevy, 59
No. 18 *Small Soldiers* Pontiac, 99
No. 25 Coast Guard bank set, 49
No. 28 Texaco, 68
No. 33 Skoal Monte Carlo, 14
No. 35 Tabasco Pontiac, 12
No. 40 Coors Chevy, 14

Revell-Monogram
1996 No. 88 Quality Care T-Bird, 73
1997 John Deere Grand Prix, 82
1997 No. 24 Jurassic Park Chevy, 45
1997 No. 31 Lowe's Chevy, 58
No. 97 John Deere Pontiac, 24

Revell Select
No. 25 Budweiser Monte Carlo, 48
1997 No. 97 John Deere Pontiac, 83

Starter
1985 No. 28 Hardee's Ford T-Bird, 64
1986 No. 27 Alugard Pontiac, 86
1987 No. 28 Texaco/Havoline, 65
1987 No. 3 Wrangler Chevy, 56
1988 No. 3 Goodwrench Monte Carlo, 56
1989 No. 26 Quaker State Buick, 71
1991 No. 3 Goodwrench Lumina, 56
No. 27 Kodiak Grand Prix, 87

Team Caliber
1998 No. 99 Exide Taurus, 79
1999 No. 12 Mobil 1 Taurus, 91
1999 No. 17 DeWalt Taurus, 80
1999 No. 43 STP/Petty Pontiac, 18
1999 No. 45 Sprint Chev, 40
1999 No. 6 Eagle One Taurus, 77
2000 No. 16 FamilyClick.com Ford, 81
2000 No. 17 DeWalt Taurus, 80
2000 No. 45 Sprint Chevy, 40
2000 No. 5 Kellogg's Chevy, 51
2000 No. 6 Eagle One Taurus, 77

Testors 1998 No. 5 Kellogg's Chevy, 50

128